PROPHECY
AND
MODERN TIMES

W. CLEON SKOUSEN

Find The Prophecy and Modern Times on Facebook
http://www.facebook.com/ ProphecyandModernTimes

Published by:
Izzard Ink, LLC
PO Box 522251
Salt Lake City, Utah 84152

Print Edition ISBN: 978-1630720667
Electronic Book ISBN: 978-1630720629

To contact W. Cleon Skousen about bulk orders or any
questions please e-mail info@wcleonskousen.com

http://www.wcleonskousen.com

IZZARD INK™
PUBLISHING

PREFACE

During the past eighteen years, while serving as a teacher in various Church auxiliaries and acting as a stake mission president, an attempt has been made to assemble all the prophecies pertaining to modern times which appear in the Bible, the Book of Mormon, the Doctrine and Covenants, the Pearl of Great Price the authoritative writings of Church leaders.

These prophecies, with footnotes, have been arranged according to the period or the subject matter to which they refer and it is the sincere hope of the author that they will thereby become more accessible to the student and more easily assimilated by those who do not have time for lengthy research.

The contents of the second and third editions are identical. However, they are considerably enlarged over the first edition which was published in December, 1939, at Washington, D.C. Additional time for research has permitted the compilation and writing of a new section entitled, "Prophecy Concerning the Millennium," which did not appear in the first edition.

With this edition, as with the other two, I wish particularly to acknowledge the faithful assistance of my wife without whose industry and research the production of this work might have been permanently postponed. I also wish to acknowledge my deep appreciation to those many friends whose interest and encouragement have facilitated the completion of this work in its final form.

"Search these commandments, for they are true and faithful, and the prophecies and promises which are in them shall all be fulfilled.

"What I the Lord have spoken, I have spoken, and I excuse not myself; and though the heavens and earth pass away, my word shall not pass away, but shall all be fulfilled whether by mine own voice or by the voice of my servants, it is the same."[1]

W. Cleon Skousen

---

1 D&C 1:37-38.

Preface to the Fifth Edition

I deeply appreciate the many new friends whom I have come to know through the intermediary of this little book. It also has been a source of hearting encouragement to see the great number of youth who are becoming careful students of the scripture. They are to be commended for their prayerful search--for it will surely help them solve the problems of their generation as it has helped their fathers solve those of the past.

W. Cleon Skousen
October 1, 1954
Provo, Utah

Forward by Ezra Taft Benson

Prophecy is a miracle of knowledge of events before they transpire. Prophecy is a history in reverse. It is neither speculation nor guessing, but it is a divine disclosure of future events through inspired instruments.

The Lord has known the end from the beginning. To His prophets He revealed the important events of this world from the very genesis until the end thereof. To Adam, Abraham, Enoch, the brother of Jared, Lehi and other prophets, the Lord has made clear His secrets and the blue-print of His plans for the Human family and all creation. To Joseph Smith, the prophet of the Dispensation of the Fullness of Times -- the greatest of all dispensations -- He said:

"Thus saith the Lord your God, even Jesus Christ, the Great I Am, Alpha and Omega, the beginning and the end, the same which looked upon the wide expanse of eternity, and all the seraphic hosts of heaven, before the world was made;

"The same which knoweth all things, for all things are present before mine eyes;

"I am the same which spake, and the world was made, and all things came by me."[2]

Prophecy is recognized as a characteristic feature of the ministry in a Gospel Dispensation. A prophet is one who speaks for God under the inspiration of Heaven. "For the prophecy came not in old time by the will of man; but holy men of God spake as they were moved by the Holy Ghost."[2]

---

2   2 Peter 1:21

Paul declares prophecy to be one of the most desirable of all spiritual endowments.

Man has always been interested in the future. This has led to extended speculation, much of which has been fruitless and even harmful. The history of humanity has, to a large extent, been one of groping blindly in the dark, fearing for the future and yet resisting the guiding hand of inspired men who would willingly lead mankind in the path of safety. While ever seeking happiness, they have pursued their own willful ways, attempting shortcuts and trying panaceas, paying little or no attention to the more sure word of prophecy. As a result man has felt little security as he has attempted to scan the future. His plans have been uncertain and his heart filled with anxiety.

Through the ages a kind Heavenly Father, loving His children, has pointed the way and endeavored to persuade them to hearken to the word of prophecy and escape the ills which men heap upon themselves. He has offered the enjoyment of peace of mind, security, prosperity and exaltation through obedience. At the same time, He has pointed out the disastrous results of failure to heed the warnings of the prophets.

Yes, the prophets of God have had vital messages for us in the past, as they have in the critical days of the present. In the even more critical days of the future, we will do well to heed their counsel. Had we understood and believed their words in the past, many of our difficulties might have been averted. It is well that we give sincere and prayerful consideration to the great prophecies yet to be fulfilled in the days immediately ahead -- in modern times. It is these prophecies which have in them so much of interest and value to the people of our day. It behooves all to give prayerful study and attention to the inspired word of prophecy as we anxiously face an uncertain future, ever remembering the Lord's word to the prophet Amos, that "Surely the Lord God will do nothing, but he revealeth his secret unto his servants the prophets."[3]

It is to this difficult but challenging task of making such study easier and more fruitful that Elder W. Cleon Skousen has set his hand. The study has consumed much of the time that could be snatched from a busy professional and active church service. It has been an unselfish labor by one who loves the Word of the Lord.

Within these covers Elder Skousen has brought together prophecies bearing on modern times, which he discusses in an uncompromising and forthright manner. Every person interested in present and future events in this war-torn world will profit from a careful perusal of these pages. The author speaks out of a rich life as student of the scriptures, ardent missionary and popular teacher. His compilation, orderly arrangement and comment on the prophecies pertaining to our day will prove a valuable and worthwhile contribution to the religious literature of modern times.

May all those who read these pages be impressed with the goodness of the Lord to His children, the infallibility of His inspired word and the importance of living in accordance with the truths herein proclaimed.

---

3   Amos 3:8

Contents

PREFACE

PART I
INTRODUCTION

PART II
PROPHECY CONCERNING AMERICA

PART III
PROPHECY CONCERNING PALESTINE

PART IV
PROPHECY CONCERNING THE MILLENNIUM

PART I
INTRODUCTION

A Remarkable Prophecy in 1832

During 1830-1831, the feature stories of the American press carried news of a threatened civil war. The controversy was over the question of "Nullification." Did South Carolina have the right to nullify the new Federal tariff law? The obvious effect of such a right would be the annihilation of the powers of Congress. If South Carolina could nullify a Federal law, so could other states. It would be the end of the Union.

Andrew Jackson was President and the political leaders of all parties waited anxiously to see what he would do. If he bowed meekly to this spirit of rebellion, other states would follow. If he dispatched an army to South Carolina to enforce the Federal law, many predicted strong and immediate military resistance.

President Jackson was not a "church" man but he was a praying man. In this moment of national crisis he was pleading for divine guidance. Would there be civil war? What could he do to avoid it?

The President did not ask for a revelation, merely wisdom. As subsequent events clearly proved, his prayers were answered. His "wisdom" averted civil war in the United States for a whole generation.

But the prayers of President Jackson were more completely though indirectly answered through a divine manifestation which warned the people of the United States that eventually civil war would engulf the nation. The revelation was not received in the White House nor did it come to the President. It came to a humble young man, twenty-seven years of age, who was residing at Kirtland, Ohio. His name

14

was Joseph Smith.

It was Christmas day, 1832, nearly three years after the famous debate on "Nullification" between Webster and Hayne that Joseph Smith received the answer to the most provoking and dynamic issue in the nation:

"Thus saith the Lord concerning the wars that will shortly come to pass, beginning at the rebellion of South Carolina, which will eventually terminate in the death and misery of many souls.... For behold, the Southern States shall be divided against the Northern States, and the Southern States will call on other nations, even the nation of Great Britain as it is called, and they shall also call upon other nations in order to defend themselves.... And it shall come to pass after many days, slaves shall rise up against their masters, who shall be marshaled and disciplined for war."[4]

On December 25, 1832, Joseph Smith therefore knew six specific things which the Lord had decreed would shortly come to pass:

1. That in spite of the President's efforts there would be a civil war in the United States.

2. That it would begin with the rebellion of South Carolina.

3. That the spirit of rebellion would spread among the "Southern States" until they divided against the Northern States.

4. That it would be a war of major proportions resulting in the death and misery of many souls.

5. That the Southern States would call on foreign nations, including Great Britain, to assist them in their cause.

4   D&C 87:1-4.

6. That slavery rather than "nullification" would be the issue and that slaves would rise against their masters and be marshaled for war.

How to Interpret Prophecy

There are two significant things which this prophecy illustrates. First, the Lord rarely, if ever, signifies the exact date when a prediction will come to pass. He will disclose the period and the accompanying circumstances but not the precise date.

In fact, almost immediately after this prophecy was given, the clouds of threatened civil strife began to dissipate themselves. The Presidents vigorous action against South Carolina seemed to dam the tide of rebellion. By the end of the famous "Jacksonian Era" there was little fear remaining in the minds of most people concerning further difficulty. The threat civil war was generally considered a dead issue.

Nevertheless, the Lord's declaration stood.

The second thing to note in connection with this prophecy is that when it was finally fulfilled, it was fulfilled to the very letter. It requires no stretching of the imagination or history to make the facts literally fit the prediction.

Not only is this characteristic true of the above prophecy, it is likewise true of all prophecy. As we look back down the corridors of the past we find that every prophetic declaration authorized by heaven has been literally fulfilled. The Great Flood was literal. The crucifixion of the Lord was literal. And so was the destruction of Jerusalem. Prophecy is not poetry. It is history in reverse. It needs no private interpretation. It is fulfilled literally.

In the following pages we will therefore keep these two

keys of interpretation in mind: First, that anyone attempting to apply a mathematical formula to prophecy so as to fix exact dates is operating outside of the prophetic pattern which the Lord has laid down. He gives us the season, but not the date. Secondly, whatever the Lord has declared concerning the past was literally fulfilled. We may reasonably expect the same of all prophecies dealing with the future.

The Purpose of Prophecy

The purpose of prophecy is frequently misunderstood. It is not the Lord's purpose to completely remove the veil which guards the future. Too much prophecy would defeat the plan of salvation. Life on earth was designed for our education and testing. As Jehovah declared concerning the earth before it was made:

"We will go down, for there is space there, and we will take of these materials and we will make an earth whereon these may dwell; and we will prove them herewith, to see if they will do all things whatsoever the Lord their God shall command them."[5]

Prophecy is usually in the form of a conditional promise of reward or punishment designed to determine whether or not we will do whatsoever thing the Lord commands us. In revealing the future the Lord has exercised great care. To reveal too much would inevitably overwhelm the free agency of man and deprive us of our chance to choose. If the Lord revealed the answer to every whimsical problem arising in our lives there certainly would be no testing of the human family and practically no learning. Therefore the Lord has warned his children not to ask for prophecy or revelation on minor matters:

"For behold, it is not meet that I should command in all

_____
5   Abraham 3:24-25.

things; for he that is compelled in all things, the same is a slothful and not a wise servant; wherefore he receiveth no reward.

"Verily, I say, men should be anxiously engaged in a good cause, and do many things of their own free will ... for the power is in them wherein they are agents unto themselves."[6]

There are some people who are not satisfied with heavenly principles to live by; they demand specific guidance for every specific problem. These are they who go out after fortune tellers, crystal gazers, familiar spirits or pseudo-psychic sooth-sayers who are as ignorant of the answers as they themselves, but who will gladly take a chance at guessing for a price.

Prophecy, however, is not guessing. Nor is it speculation. Prophecy is a divine disclosure of future events -- events of which our Heavenly Father already has present and certain knowledge.

Prophecy Based Upon a Scientific Principle

There is no mystery in God's capacity to know future events with certainty. Even men enjoy this ability to a limited extent. It is an attribute which is simply dependent upon knowledge of all the controlling factors leading up to any particular event. God, who is familiar with every influence in the cosmic universe, finds no difficulty in predetermining what will happen at any time or with any set of circumstances.

This certainty of foreknowledge grows with experience and planning.

6 D&C 58:26-28.

The Lord states that this earth is only one of countless planets which he has embellished with human, plant and animal life.[7] Like a laboratory experiment that has been performed an infinite number of times, the omniscient Master Technician can foretell from moment to moment what to expect.

The Lord also informs us that a complete and detailed blueprint for this earth's function as a home for the human family was worked out in advance.[8] And the part each human being would play was worked out on the basis of God's foreknowledge of how each one of us would conduct ourselves under certain conditions. Thus, in the morning of creation, God was able to reveal to Adam "whatsoever should befall his posterity unto the latest generation."[9] And Nephi said: "The Lord knoweth all things from the beginning."[10]

Members of Church Expected to Know Prophecy and Its Fulfillment

"And I give unto you a commandment that you shall teach one another the doctrine of the kingdom. Teach diligently and my grace shall attend you, that you may be instructed more perfectly in theory, in principle, in doctrine, in the law of the gospel, in all things that pertain unto the kingdom of God that are expedient for you to understand; of things both in heaven and in earth, and under the earth; things which have been, things which are, things which must shortly come to pass; things which are at home, things which are abroad; the wars and the perplexities of the nations, and the judgments which are on the land; and a knowledge also of countries and of kingdoms -- that ye

---

7   Moses 1:35.
8   Abraham 5:3
9   D&C 107:56.
10 1 Nephi 9:6.

may be prepared in all things when I shall send you again to magnify the calling whereunto I have called you, and the mission with which I have commissioned you."[11]

Our Day Anticipated by All the Prophets

It should be of particular significance to all those who profess a sincere interest in the scriptures to know that God revealed more to his prophets concerning the happening of events in our day than he has concerning any other period in the history of mankind. This is the sixtieth century in the history of Adam's children of which "God hath spoken by the mouth of all the holy prophets since the world began."[12]

Concerning it, the Prophet Joseph Smith had this to say:

"It is a theme upon which prophets, priests and kings have dwelt with peculiar delight; they have looked forward with joyful anticipation to the day in which we live; and fired with heavenly and joyful anticipations they have sung and written and prophesied of this our day. But they died without the sight. We are the favored people that God has made choice of to bring about the latter-day glory. It is left for us to see, participate in and help roll forward the latter-day glory -- `the dispensation of the fullness of times when God will gather together all things that are in heaven and all things that are upon the earth,' `even in one'; when the Saints of God will be gathered in one from every nation, and kindred, and people, and tongue when the Jews will be gathered together into one, the wicked will also be gathered together to be destroyed as spoken of by the prophets; the Spirit of God will also dwell with his people, and be withdrawn from the rest of the nations, and all things whether in heaven or on earth will be in one, even in Christ.

---

11   D&C 88:77-80.
12   Acts 3:21.

"The heavenly Priesthood will unite with the earthly to bring about those great purposes; and whilst we are thus united in one common cause, to roll forth the Kingdom of God, the heavenly Priesthood are not idle spectators.

"The Spirit of God will be showered down from above, and it will dwell in our midst. The blessings of the Most High will rest upon our tabernacles and our name will be handed down to future ages. Our children will rise up and call us blessed, and generations yet unborn will dwell with peculiar delight upon the scenes that we have passed through -- the privations that we have endured, the untiring zeal that we have manifested, the all but insurmountable difficulties that we have overcome in laying the foundation of a work that brought about the glory and blessing which they will realize; a work that God and angels have contemplated with delight for generations past; that fired the souls of the ancient patriarchs and prophets; a work that is destined to bring about the destruction of the powers of darkness, the renovation of the earth, the glory of God and the salvation of the human family."[13]

In contemplation of our dispensation the prophets reached across the centuries to tell us of the great events that would mark our day among the seasons of eternity. Thus, the following pages are a compilation of the ancient and modern prophecies as they relate to our times and our lives. In the program of the Lord, we have a part -- it may become a most important part. The prophets wrote, therefore, to warn us and to teach us that we might perform our parts intelligently and well.

---

13   Teachings of the Prophet Joseph Smith, p. 231.

PART II
PROPHECY CONCERNING AMERICA

Prophecy Concerning America

It should animate the soul of every American to know that nearly all of the major events in the historical development of North and South America were revealed by the Lord to his prophet's ages ago.

One prophet was shown the discoverer of America. He saw him leave Europe, sail across the Atlantic and discover this continent through the guidance and inspiration of the Lord.[14] This prophet knew that the first Europeans to reach America would find native inhabitants in great numbers,[15] and another prophet said these aborigines would be loathsome and dark-skinned -- a people practicing idolatry.[16]

Immediately following the discovery of America, a spirit of conquest and exploitation was breathed out against this land by the quarreling, greedy kings of Europe. Up until the second quarter of the nineteenth century it was a foregone conclusion that eventually the Americas would be divided among them. But the word of prophecy was against it. More than five hundred years before the birth of Christ, the Lord revealed to one of his prophets that no king -- whether from Europe, Asia, or the islands of the sea -- would succeed in securing a permanent foothold on this land in our day.[17]

America was predestined by the Lord to be a land of freedom and refuge. One of the prophets was shown the Pilgrim Fathers and multitudes of persecuted people immigrating to America to escape the "captivity" and afflictions of Europe.[18]

---

14   1 Nephi 13:12.
15   1 Nephi 13:12.
16   Mormon 5:15.
17   2 Nephi 10:10-13.
18   1 Nephi 13:13, 19.

He predicted the American Revolution 2,300 years before it occurred and knew the American colonies would win it.[19]

A Senator vs. the Prophets

In the trying days of early American history there were many important leaders who refused to believe that the massive and rugged American continent could ever attain an enviable destiny. This sentiment found expression as late as 1845 when Senator George H. McDuffie of South Carolina bristled at the thought of further western expansion. Referring to the agricultural possibilities in the region of the west coast, he emphatically declared:

"Why sir ... I would not for that purpose give a pinch of snuff for the whole territory. I wish to God we did not own it."[20]

In reply to the Senator there is a prophetic refutation by an angel of the Lord who announced nearly six hundred years before the meridian of time that the land of America should be "choice above all other lands," and that in our day the God of Heaven would raise up a gentile nation upon it that would be "above all other nations."[21]

We who live only a century later see the word of the Lord literally fulfilled while the words of the Senator from South Carolina lie wholly refuted by the preponderant evidence of American history.

American Indian and the Bible in Prophecy

Not only did the prophets foretell the rise of a mighty

---

19   1 Nephi 13:17-19.
20   Congressional Globe, 27th Congress, 3rd Session, pp.198-201.
21   1 Nephi 13:30.

gentile people on the American continent, but they predicted the downfall of all the so-called "Indian" nations.

Who but inspired servants of the Lord could have anticipated centuries ago that a man like Hernando Cortez, for example, with only eleven ships, four hundred Europeans, two hundred natives, sixteen horses and fourteen guns, could have attacked, plundered and massacred into subjugation an empire of several million Aztecs. Or that a man like Francisco Pizarro with a starved and desperate band of a hundred and sixty-eight Spaniards could have taken possession of the entire kingdom belonging to the ancient empire of the Incas.

The prophets said that men such as these would pour out their wrath on the Indian nations, scattering and driving them like a whirlwind.[22]

Nevertheless, the scripture promises that "God will not suffer that the gentiles will utterly destroy" the Indians.[23] Eventually, as we shall discuss later, the Indian people are to enjoy a position of respectable prominence among the inhabitants of this land.

Culturally speaking, the prophets knew that in the warp and woof of our national life the Bible would have a prominent place.[24] But the Lord revealed to Moses that many parts of it would be changed or lost[25] and he revealed to the Apostle Peter that the people of our day would not believe the contents of the Bible.[26] Peter said they would be "willingly" ignorant of its historical value, denying the story of the Great Flood, for example, and saying: "All things continue as they were from the beginning of the creation." This is a singular

22 1 Nephi 13:14; 3 Nephi 16:8-9; 1 Nephi 22:7.
23 1 Nephi 13:30.
24 2 Nephi 29:3-13; 1 Nephi 13:38.
25 Moses 1:41.
26 2 Peter 3:1-6.

prophecy. Consider the great modern paradox wherein the people of this and other nations buy up more copies of the Bible than any other published volume, and yet, in the final analysis, do not believe in it!

Importance of American History

Why were the prophets of old concerned with early American history? What was there about those early scenes of discovery, conquest and revolution -- followed eventually by a stable form of government -- which made America different from similar scenes in the opening up of other new lands?

Superficially there does not appear to be any innate quality in the history of the Western Hemisphere which would warrant having the Lord presents it in panoramic vision to his prophet's centuries ago. And yet, even as such a conclusion is reached, the Lord answers it through the writings of a score of prophets.

The history of America is important because it is interwoven with significant developments in the Pre-Millennial preparation of the earth by the Lord.

As the flood water in the days of Noah withdrew from the highlands of North and South America, the Lord declared this hemisphere to be a land of destiny on which he would build the world's most glorious capital -- the New Jerusalem.[27] Therefore, the opening scenes of American history were impregnated with the foundation stones which the Lord himself has been carefully laying preparatory to the erecting of a superstructure of celestial government upon the earth.

This is the age concerning which God has spoken by all

_____
27   Ether 13:2-8.

his holy prophets, and they foresaw the work of the Lord growing contemporaneously with the discovery and development of this land.

The presence of the Lord moving in the early scenes of American history made it a fit subject for prophetic utterances.

Little Known Facts Concerning America Revealed

Geographically, no portion of the earth has been endowed with a more dramatic and interesting place in the pageant of human life upon the earth than the American continent.

Until modern revelation disclosed it, the real history of the western hemisphere lay buried in the labyrinth of the forgotten past. Consider, for example, the thrilling disclosure that human life had its beginning on this continent. After centuries of academic speculation, the Lord finally revealed that the Garden of Eden was not in Mesopotamia as many had supposed, but here in North America.[28]

It was here that Adam lived and the entire antediluvian civilization was established.[29] It was here that the City of Enoch was built. This was where Methuselah lived nine hundred and sixty-nine years and where his grandson Noah, built the historic Ark preparatory to the Great Flood.[30]

As every Bible student knows, the Ark rode the great deep for approximately five months and then came to rest on Mount Ararat[31] and when the flood waters had subsided

---

28   Matthias F. Cowley, Wilford Woodruff, p. 481.
29   D&C 107:53 and D&C 116.
30   Joseph Fielding Smith, The Progress of Man, p. 249.
31   Genesis 8:4.

Noah's immediate descendants settled in the Mesopotamian Valley.[32] In doing so, they followed the natural inclination to name rivers, mountains, valleys and territories after those they had known in their former homeland. A large river was named "Euphrates." One area was named "Canaan," another "Ethiopia." These, however, were all names which originally belonged to geographical locations in America.[33]

America Repopulated After the Flood

The Great Flood destroyed all human and animal life on the American continent, but in the Book of Ether the Lord reveals that almost immediately after the deluge, a choice group of Noah's descendants were led back to America to repopulate it. They were called the "People of Jared."

They brought with them all kinds of animals,[34] and eight boats were required to bring them across the ocean.[35]

This people established a marvelous civilization which, according to the Lord, was greater than any contemporary kingdom.[36] This would include the Babylonian, Assyrian, Chinese and Egyptian civilizations.

The Jaredites existed on the American continent from approximately 2300 to 600 B.C. when they annihilated themselves through civil war.

Lehi's Colony from Jerusalem

In 600 B.C. the Lord anticipated the destruction of the Jaredites in America by commanding the Prophet Lehi who

32   Genesis 11:2.
33   Moses 3:13-14, 7:7.
34   Ether 2:1-3.
35   Ether 3:1.
36   Ether 1:43.

was living in Jerusalem to take a small colony of people and follow the course of travel which would be revealed to him. This group of people took an overland route across Arabia, and after reaching the seashore constructed a ship in which they successfully negotiated the trans-oceanic voyage to America.[37] The entire history of this people is contained in the Book of Mormon.

Lehi and his little band of followers landed far south of the Jaredite Empire, but several generations later Lehi's descendants stumbled onto the ruins of that former civilization.

In the meantime, however, the descendants of Lehi had divided into two separate nations. During the next thousand years they grew until their buildings and cities covered "the whole face of the land."[38] It was in the fourth century A.D. that these two great nations met head on in a gigantic military conflict which lasted sixty years and resulted in the annihilation of the Nephite nation which was the more enlightened segment of Lehi's progeny.

The victors in this conflict were known as the Lamanites and were the ancestors of the modern American Indian. But never again did they regain their former dignity and refinement. They degenerated into numerous primitive tribal societies which continued up until the discovery of America by Columbus. Today, these American aborigines retain only a crude and obscure tradition concerning the majestic splendor of their former greatness.

Thus it will be seen that the American continent has been inhabited almost continuously since man first became a resident upon the earth.

---

37   See the Book of 1 Nephi.
38   Mormon 1:7.

It will also be observed that practically none of America's ancient history has been known until recent times when the Lord himself revealed it. This was done that we might better appreciate the significance of events occurring on this land today. Not only has America been the scene for much of man's epic achievements and experiences in the past, but it is also the land on which the Lord determined to initiate his great Pre-Millennial program in the last days.

Centuries ago the Lord described in remarkable detail the highlights of his work which he would commence on this continent in our time.

Our Dispensation in Prophecy

All those who are familiar with the work of the Lord in this day marvel that he should have revealed so many details concerning it to his prophets of old. The mission of Joseph Smith, for example, was well known among the prophets hundreds of years before he was born. They knew what his name would be,[39] and the magnitude of the work he would perform.[40] Malachi called him a messenger.[41] Isaiah knew that he would be unlearned after the manner of men.[42] To Jeremiah he was a latter-day pastor who would feed the Saints with knowledge and understanding,[43] and Moses was told that he would be a mighty prophet like unto him.[44]

Joseph who was sold into Egypt knew that the prophet raised up in the last days would be one of his own descendants and that he and his father would both bear the name

---

39   2 Nephi 3:6, 15.
40   2 Nephi 3:24.
41   Malachi 3:1; Parley P. Pratt, Key to Theology, p. 79.
42   Isaiah 29:12.
43   Jeremiah 3:14-15.
44   Moses 1:41.

of Joseph.[45] About 400 A.D. Moroni wrote down a whole chapter of instructions specifically addressed to him,[46] The Prophet Nephi spoke plainly concerning him,[47] and when the Messiah came to the American continent immediately after his resurrection, he told the Nephites of the great prophet he would raise up in our day.[48]

The coming forth of the Book of Mormon was likewise familiar to many early prophets. Joseph, the favorite son of Jacob, predicted it.[49] Ezekiel had a revelation concerning it.[50] Enoch was told that it would come forth out of the earth and bear testimony to the divinity and resurrection of the Messiah.[51] Moroni recorded that no man on earth in our day would be able to translate it except a prophet of the Lord having a "means for the interpretation thereof."[52]

Nephi knew that a major portion of the plates would be sealed,[53] and Isaiah commented on this fact saying that a scientist would remark that he couldn't translate a sealed book.[54] Then Isaiah said that the unlearned prophet of the Lord would translate it to the confounding of the wise.[55]

Nephi knew that Joseph Smith would not be permitted to show the plates of Mormon to any save a few select witnesses who could testify of their authenticity.[56] He knew

---

45   2 Nephi 3:6, 15.
46   Ether, Chapter 5.
47   2 Nephi 27:9-12.
48   3 Nephi 21, 9-11.
49   2 Nephi 3:7, 11-12.
50   Ezekiel 37:15-20.
51   Moses 7:62.
52   Mormon 9:34.
53   2 Nephi 27:22.
54   Isaiah 29:11.
55   Isaiah 29:14.
56   2 Nephi 27:12-13.

that the people in our day would resent the coming forth of another sacred scripture even though it contained precious truths that had previously been lost. "A Bible! A Bible!" they would cry; "We have got a Bible and there cannot be any more Bible."[57] And this they would cry out, said Nephi, even though they did not believe in the Bible nor understand it.

The ancient prophets also saw the restoration of the Church of Christ upon the earth and the practical results which would follow. The Messiah declared that the work of the Church in the last days would be of world-wide proportions,[58] but he revealed to Nephi that the actual membership of the Church would be small.[59] While John was in vision of the Isle of Patmos, he saw Moroni, the angelic harbinger, declaring the good news of the restored gospel,[60] and Lehi saw the Lord gathering out the Saints through the work of the Prophet Joseph.[61]

Isaiah said that the Saints would be Israelites and become known and honored as such among the gentiles.[62] Thus Isaiah knew that the choice seed of Ephraim would be raised up;[63] that today the fifty million Lamanites or Indians who are descendants of Manasseh would be identified with Israel and that through the Book of Mormon their history and former blessings would be revealed as by a voice from the dust.[64] He knew that the great lost tribes of Israel would be brought down again from the north[65] and that the scattered

---

57　2 Nephi 29:3.
58　Matthew 24:14.
59　1 Nephi 14:12; 2 Nephi 28:14.
60　Revelation 14:6-7 plus D&C 133:36.
61　2 Nephi 3:24.
62　Isaiah 61:9; Zephaniah 3:19.
63　Isaiah 11:13.
64　Isaiah 11:11 plus 1 Nephi 22:1-6 and 2 Nephi 27:9.
65　Isaiah 11:16.

Hebrew nation would again become a united people.[66]

All this was to come to pass to permit the God of Sabaoth to re-establish his covenant among his chosen people.[67]

While Jesus was ministering among the Jews, he indicated that John the Baptist would assist in the restoration of the gospel prior to the coming of the Lord in power,[68] and Malachi predicted that Elijah would also participate.[69]

Ezekiel saw the Church assembled in the wilderness where the Lord would show forth a great revelation, purge out the rebels, renew the everlasting covenant, and talk with the Saints face to face.[70] This, said Daniel, will be the final restoration of the Church and Kingdom of God on the earth. It shall never again be destroyed.[71]

Zion in the Mountains

Although Ezekiel speaks of the people of Israel being taken into the wilderness to receive their covenant and a new revelation, this was not where they were to remain. Eventually, they were to go up into the mountains.

This phase of Church history is frequently referred to by Isaiah who closely associates the hills and mountains with the bringing forth of the kingdom of Zion in the latter days. He exclaims: "O Zion, that bringest good tidings, get thee up into the high mountain."[72] He also predicts, as does the Prophet Micah, that the Lord's house should be built in the

---

66   Isaiah 11:12; 52:9; Joel 3:20.
67   Jeremiah 31:31; Romans 11:26-27.
68   Matthew 17:11-13.
69   Malachi 4:5.
70   Ezekiel 20:34-38.
71   Daniel 2:44.
72   Isaiah 40:9.

mountains.[73] Isaiah stated that the righteous of Zion would dwell in high places, in a land that was "very far off," and that their defenses would be "the munitions of rocks."[74] An angel of the Lord declared unto Nephi that the missionaries who proclaimed the message of Zion in the last days would be "beautiful upon the mountains."[75]

It is the testimony of the Church of Jesus Christ now upon the earth that all these prophecies have been or are in process of being fulfilled. The Saints have seen the body of the Church driven forth from wilderness to wilderness and have finally seen her go up into the high mountains where the rocks were her defense and where temples could be built unto the Lord.

Will the Church Headquarters Remain in the Mountains?

The spirit of prophecy has whispered that the headquarters of the Church cannot always remain in the mountains; however it is in Jackson County, Missouri, that the Center Stake will be built.[76] That is a place choice unto the Lord where Adam himself once lived and which God called the Garden of Eden.[77] It is the place to which the Saints now look for the voice of the Lord will yet call them out and lead them back to that sacred portion of the earth destined for the Center Stake of Zion, the New Jerusalem.

Orson F. Whitney understood the movement of Zion from the mountains and said: "Will our mission end here (in Utah)? Is the State of Utah the proper monument of the Mormon people? No.... The monument to Mormonism will

---

73   Isaiah 2:2-3; Micah 4:1-2.
74   Isaiah 33:15-17.
75   1 Nephi 13:37.
76   Discourse of Brigham Young, page 174.
77   Matthias F. Cowley, Wilford Woodruff, p. 481.

stand in Jackson County, Missouri. There the great City will be built: There Zion will arise and shine, `the joy of the whole earth,' and there the Lord will come to his temple in his own time, when his people shall have made the required preparation."[78]

The Prophecy of Heber C. Kimball

This great movement from the mountains to the place of the New Jerusalem will be a glorious mission unto those who are found worthy to be ordained and sent, but the voice of prophecy warns us that the circumstances which immediately precede this event will be heavy laden with tribulation for the weary and a quagmire for the unwary.

Consider the words of President Heber C. Kimball as he viewed the events of that future day.

"An army of Elders will be sent to the four quarters of the earth to search out the righteous and warn the wicked of what is coming. All kinds of religions will be started and miracles performed that will deceive the very elect if that were possible. Our sons and daughters must live pure lives so as to be prepared for what is coming.

"After a while the gentiles will gather by the thousands to this place, and Salt Lake City will be classed among the wicked cities of the world. A spirit of speculation and extravagance will take possession of the Saints, and the results will be financial bondage.

"Persecution comes next and all true Latter-day Saints will be tested to the limit. Many will apostatize and others will still not know what to do. Darkness will cover the earth and gross darkness the minds of the people. The judgments of God will be poured out on the wicked to the extent that

78   D&C Commentary, page 196.

our Elders from far and near will be called home, or in other words the gospel will be taken from the Gentiles and later on carried to the Jews.

"The western boundary of the State of Missouri will be swept so clean of its inhabitants that as President Young tells us, when you return to that place, there will not be left so much as a yellow dog to wag his tail.

"Before that day comes, however, the Saints will be put to tests that will try the integrity of the best of them. The pressure will become so great that the more righteous among them will cry unto the Lord day and night until deliverance comes.

"Then the prophet and others will make their appearance and those who have remained faithful will be selected to return to Jackson County, Missouri, and take part in the up building of that beautiful city, the New Jerusalem."[79]

The spirit of President Kimball reminds one of Nephi who said: "For behold, my soul delighteth in plainness unto my people, that they may learn.... And now, my brethren, I have spoken plainly that ye cannot err."[80]

Brother Kimball speaks of the time when the western boundaries of Missouri will be swept clean of its inhabitants. He speaks of a future persecution of the Saints, and he refers to the time when the Elders of the Church will be called home from far and near. Not only will they be called home from foreign nations, but from the American gentile nations as well.

_____ Prophecies Relating to

79   Deseret News, May 23, 1931.
80   2 Nephi 25:4, 20.

Future Events in America

The word of the Lord is sure, and the above quotation of President Kimball together with other related prophecies emphatically declare that if the gentiles who now inhabit this promised land ever take it upon themselves to utterly reject the basic ethics of Christianity and resist the latter-day work -- driving the Saints so that they "cry unto the Lord day and night" -- then the restored gospel of peace will be withdrawn from among them. A multitude of prophecies -- particularly those contained in the Book of Mormon -- hiss forth a warning to the American gentiles.

When the Savior visited the Nephites following his resurrection he promised that the gentiles who discovered and populated the American continent in the last days would be allowed, together with their children, to possess the land forever, provided they remained humble and did not utterly reject the mission of the latter-day Church which the Lord promised he would raise up in their midst.[81] He even promised that if they were faithful the American gentiles of the last days would be given the privilege of assisting in building the New Jerusalem.[82]

However, there is a great responsibility placed upon all those who enjoy the choice blessing of living in America in our day. The Prophet Lehi, who brought a colony out of Jerusalem to America in the sixth century before Christ, looked down through the corridors of passing time and declared:

"Wherefore, I, Lehi, prophesy according to the workings of the Spirit which is in me, that there shall none come into this land save they shall be brought by the hand of the Lord.

---

81   3 Nephi 21:22-24.
82   3 Nephi 21:22-24.

"Wherefore, this land is consecrated unto him whom he shall bring. And if it so be that they shall serve him according to the commandments which he hath given, it shall be a land of liberty unto them; wherefore, they shall never be brought down into captivity; if so, it shall be because of iniquity; for if iniquity shall abound, cursed shall be the land for their sakes, but unto the righteous it shall be blessed forever."[83]

Thus, two great prophecies rest upon the gentiles of this land. They will choose one or the other. If they choose righteousness, they and their children will be blessed here forever. But if they choose wickedness then the Lord clearly predicts what they may expect.

First, he declared that they would become so great -- so politically powerful and economically prosperous -- that their pride would be lifted up "above all nations, and above all the people of the whole earth."[84]

Second, he predicted that they would become a nation of liars, hypocrites and murderers; addicted to all manner of licentiousness and practicing fraud upon one another through secret combinations.[85]

The Savior further recorded the warning that if these conditions should be permitted to exist among the American gentiles of the latter day, the cup of his indignation and wrath would overflow against them. He said the gospel would be taken from among them[86] and he would then let loose the forces that would "cut them off" from the face of the land.[87]

---

83   2 Nephi 1:6-7.
84   3 Nephi 16:10.
85   3 Nephi 16:10.
86   3 Nephi 16:10.
87   3 Nephi 21:11, 20.

How Would This Prophecy Be Fulfilled?

Surely, no man could of himself anticipate the source of the power which the Lord would use against the gentiles of this continent if their conduct should arouse the indignation and wrath of heaven.

Behold, saith the Lord, it will be the lowly Lamanites -- the very people whom the American gentiles have trodden under and scattered -- the people whom the Lord refers to as "a remnant of Jacob." It was predicted centuries ago that although the American gentiles would scatter the Indians and make them a hiss and a byword,[88] yet they would arise to become the terror of their conquerors in the day of the Lord's wrath.[89]

Here are the words of the Savior to the progenitors of the American Indian when he taught them during his visit to this hemisphere shortly after his resurrection:

"And thus commandeth the Father that I should say unto you: At that day when the Gentiles shall sin against my gospel, and shall be lifted up in the pride of their hearts above all nations, and above all the people of the whole earth, and shall be filled with all manner of lyings and of deceits, and of mischiefs, and all manner of hypocrisy, and murders, and priest crafts, and whoredoms, and of secret abominations ... and shall reject the fullness of my gospel, behold, saith the Father, I will bring the fullness of my gospel from among them," for "if the Gentiles do not repent after the blessing which they shall receive, after they have scattered my people -- then shall ye who are a remnant of the house of Jacob go forth among them; and ye shall be in the midst of them who shall be many; and ye shall be among them as a lion among the beasts of the forest, and as a young

88   3 Nephi 21:11, 20.
89   3 Nephi 16:15; 20:15-17; 21:12.

lion among the flocks of sheep, who if he goeth through both treadeth down and teareth in pieces, and none can deliver. Thy hand shall be lifted up upon thine adversaries, and all thine enemies shall be cut off."[90]

The Lord made it clear that if the Lamanites were required to cleanse the land of gentile wickedness it would be prior to the conversion of the Lamanites to the Gospel. He stated that if such a cleansing became necessary, the gentiles would be "cut off" prior to the building the New Jerusalem,[91] then he explained that after that great city had been built the Savior would personally reign over his people and personally supervise the converting and gathering in of the Lamanites.[92]

The fact that the Lamanites will not yet have been converted to the gospel when they are called upon to challenge the wickedness and power of the gentiles accounts perhaps for the unparalleled fury and violence which they are described as using.[93]

There are many significant prophecies the Savior in the Book of Mormon which relate to the "gentiles" and the manner in which they shall be driven by the "remnant of Jacob" if they become wicked. A careful study of these passages will disclose that the Lord is speaking of the Lamanites when he says the "remnant of Jacob" and he is speaking principally of the American gentiles when he refers to the "gentiles." The Lord also refers occasionally to the general destruction of all gentile nations who do not repent, but the main burden of the prophecies found in Third Nephi relate principally to the American gentiles. It will be seen in Part II of this present writing that the destruction of the gentiles

90   3 Nephi 16:10; 20:15-17.
91   3 Nephi 21:15-23.
92   3 Nephi 21:23, 25, 26.
93   See 3 Nephi 21:21.

in Europe and Asia will not be by "a remnant of Jacob," but by a sudden showing forth of the power of the Lord in the elements of the earth. It is in America that the gentiles will feel the power of the "remnant of Jacob" and Mormon, seeing our day, warned the gentiles of today when he said: "Oh ye Gentiles.... Know ye not that ye are in the hands of God? Therefore, repent ye, and humble yourselves before him, lest he shall come out in justice against you -- lest a remnant of the seed of Jacob shall go forth among you as a lion, and tear you to pieces."[94]

In connection with this prophecy the Savior forewarned of a complete political and economic collapse for the gentiles of the land if they became a wicked and degenerate nation. The Lord said they would be deprived of their means of transportation, their chariots would be destroyed, their strongholds and fortresses would be torn to pieces and their mighty cities would be made a desolation.[95]

He said that the destruction of the gentiles would be so complete that every aspect of the wickedness that characterized their civilization would be done away with,[96] and that they would be cut out from among the people of the Lord.[97]

It is no wonder then that the leaders of the Church in this dispensation have labored with such indefatigable vigor and zeal to warn the people of this land of the peril which the Lord has predicted for them if they do not accept the principles of the Gospel and observe the commandments of God.

Consider the message which Bishop Newel K. Whitney was instructed to proclaim to the larger cities of the eastern United States:

94   Mormon 5:22-24.
95   3 Nephi 21:15-20.
96   3 Nephi 21:15-20.
97   3 Nephi 21:15-20.

"Let the bishop go unto the city of New York also to the city of Albany, and also to the city of Boston, and warn the people of those cities with the sound of the gospel, with a loud voice, of the desolation and utter abolishment which await them if they do reject these things. For if they do reject these things the hour of their judgment is nigh and their house shall be left unto them desolate."[98]

And to the remainder of the Elders the Lord said:

"Go ye forth as your circumstances shall permit, in your several callings, unto the great and notable cities and villages, reproving the world in righteousness of their un-righteousness and ungodly deeds, setting forth clearly and understandingly the desolation of abomination in the last day."[99]

The Prophet Joseph Smith spoke of this coming desola-tion:

"And now I am prepared to say by the authority of Jesus Christ, that not many years shall pass away before the United States shall present such a scene of bloodshed as has not a parallel in the history of our nation; pestilence, hail, famine, and earthquake will sweep the wicked of this gen-eration from off the face of the land, to open and prepare the way for the return of the lost tribes of Israel from the north country."[100]

The Book of Mormon speaks of the time when the hosts of Israel will be gathered and shall "inherit the Gentiles and make the desolate cities to be inhabited."[101]

98   D&C 84:114-115.
99   D&C 84:117.
100   Teachings of Joseph Smith, (1938 edition) p. 17.
101   3 Nephi 22:3.

Wilford Woodruff adds his testimony:

"I warn future historians to give credence to my history; for my testimony is true, and the truth of its record will be manifest in the world to come. All the words of the Lord will be fulfilled upon the nations, which are written in this book. The American nation will be broken in pieces like a potter's vessel, and will be cast down to hell if it does not repent -- and this, because of murders, whoredoms, wickedness and all manner of abominations, for the Lord has spoken it."[102]

The Constitution to Hang by a Thread

We, who are familiar with the industry, progress and grandeur of this nation as it is now constituted, marvel at such prophecies. We may be sure, however, that the coming of such a destruction will be averted as long as there are some righteous among the people. It is when they drive the righteous from among them that the sword of the Lord shall fall. The prophets declare that if such a day comes it will be when hypocrisy, murder and secret abominations prevail throughout the land, and no doubt the patience of the intelligent and righteous would be exhausted long before the Lord finally showed forth the power of his indignation.

The Lord does not reap down a nation until it is altogether ripe unto destruction. It is not the purpose of God to destroy nations but to build them up. He desires to bless, not punish. Nevertheless, God will not be mocked, and when any people begin to glory in their wickedness -- to subvert and destroy the work of the Lord -- then he has no alternative.

As in the case of Rome, the decline begins in that hour when the cross currents of national life begin to ebb and flow with a rapidity wholly baffling to the ingenuity of human

102   Matthias F. Cowley, Wilford Woodruff, p. 500.

leadership; and because a wicked nation will not submit to divine leadership they soon become their own worst enemies. Because of distrust, jealousy and unholy ambitions among the people themselves, the very structure of their civil government soon threatens to collapse.

It is at such a time that the people begin to lose confidence in their system of government. A crisis is precipitated by the populous demanding a change. This is a typical evolution of events in a nation which is sick at heart and will not admit that its growing lethargy is the result of poison issuing from within its own members.

Such a day would literally fulfill the words of the Prophet Joseph Smith when he said that the time would come when the Constitution of the United States would hang by a thread.[103] He also said that in that hour the Elders of the Church would labor with their might to save the vestiges of democracy.[104]

Orson Hyde quotes the Prophet as having said: "If the Constitution is saved at all, it will be by the Elders of this Church."[105]

Brigham Young points out that the Constitution will never be completely destroyed, however, because "it will be held inviolate by this people (the Latter-day Saints)."[106]

It is no wonder that the Lord has taken occasion to warn this nation by ancient and modern prophets of the coming of such a history making event!

Building the New Jerusalem

103　John A. Widtsoe, Discourses of Brigham Young, p. 553.
104　Joseph Fielding Smith, The Progress of Man, p. 342
105　Joseph Fielding Smith, The Progress of Man, p. 340.
106　Joseph Fielding Smith, The Progress of Man, p. 339.

The calling of the Saints to go back to Jackson County, Missouri, to build up the Capital City of the Lord, is described as occurring after that land has been swept clean of the life that inhabited it. At that time it will be surrounded by desolated cities in which the Ten Tribes will afterwards make their habitation when they come down from the north.[107]

Such a stricken condition of the country would add greatly to the handicap of the Saints as they hasten to construct the city. But the Lord revealed to Wilford Woodruff that in building the holy temple the Saints will be given the assistance of the Lord's hosts from beyond the veil. President Woodruff writes:

"I saw a short distance from the Missouri River, where I stood, twelve men dressed in the robes of the Temple. They stood in a square nearby and I was given to understand that they represented the twelve gates of the New Jerusalem. Their hands were uplifted while they were consecrating the ground; and later they laid the corner stones of the house of God. I saw myriads of angels hovering over them, and above their heads there was a pillar-like cloud. I heard the most beautiful singing in the words: `Now is established the Kingdom of our God and his Christ, and he shall reign forever and forever, and the Kingdom shall never be thrown down, for the Saints have overcome.' I saw people coming from the river and from distant places to help build the Temple. It seemed as though there were hosts of angels helping to bring material for the construction of that building. Some were in Temple robes, and the pillar-like cloud continued to hover over the spot."[108]

The Lord revealed the consecrated spot on which the city of the New Jerusalem would be built in a revelation given in

107   3 Nephi 22:3.
108   Matthias F. Cowley, Wilford Woodruff, p. 505.

1831. It was only after the Prophet Joseph Smith had pleaded in prayer for this knowledge that it was finally revealed.[109] These are the words of the Lord:

"Hearken, O ye Elders of my Church, saith the Lord your God, who have assembled yourselves together, according to my commandments, in this land, which is the land of Missouri, which is the land which I have appointed and consecrated for the gathering of the Saints. Wherefore, this is the land of promise, and the place for the city of Zion. And thus saith the Lord your God, if you will receive wisdom here is wisdom. Behold, the place which is now called Independence is the center place; and a spot for the temple is lying westward, upon a lot which is not far from the court-house. Wherefore, it is wisdom that the land should be purchased by the Saints, and also every tract lying westward, even unto the line running directly between Jew and Gentile."[110]

In another revelation the Lord warned the Saints that the glory which would accompany the building of the New Jerusalem would not come until after much tribulation,[111] and in later years the Saints learned the meaning of these words. The spirit of mob violence and extermination drove the Saints from Jackson County and into the wilderness again and eventually into the Rocky Mountains. Now the people of the Lord await the fulfillment of his promise given in connection with the building of the New Jerusalem when he said: "Wherefore the day cometh that ye shall be crowned with much glory; the hour is not yet, but is nigh at hand."[112] And again, "I, the Lord, will hasten the city in its time, and will crown the faithful with joy and rejoicing."[113]

109   Doctrinal History of the Church, Vol. 1, p. 189; See also D&C 42:61-62.
110   D&C 57:1-5.
111   D&C 58:1, 3, 4.
112   D&C 58:4.
113   D&C 52:43.

The Great Priesthood Conference at Adam-Ondi-Ahman

With the completing of the temple in the New Jerusalem, the Lord will begin to unite his Church and Kingdom on the earth with the Kingdom of Heaven beyond the veil. This event will be inaugurated at a great priesthood conference to be held at a sacred and historical spot just a few miles north of the site for the New Jerusalem. This conference is the subject matter of an entire chapter in the writings of Elder Joseph Fielding Smith. Concerning it, he said:

"Not far from the town of Gallatin, in Davies County, Missouri, there is a place known to the people as `Spring Hill.' Here a settlement of the Saints was started in 1838. This hill is on the north of the valley through which runs Grand River, described by the Prophet Joseph as a `large, beautiful, deep and rapid stream, during the high waters of spring.' In the spring and summer the surrounding valley is most beautiful, with its scattered farms discernible as far as the eye can reach. The citizens here go about their daily tasks all unaware of the wondrous occurrences which have taken place in this beautiful valley and on this hill. They are equally oblivious to the momentous events soon to be staged there.

"When the Prophet first visited the hill he called it `Tower Hill, a name I give the place in consequence of the remains of an old Nephite altar or tower that stood there,' he wrote in his journal. By the Lord, however, this place was named `Adam-ondi-Ahman,' because, said he, `it is the place where Adam shall sit, as spoken of by Daniel the Prophet'.[114]

"Three years before the death of Adam, he called together his children, including all the faithful down to the gen-

---

114   D&C 116

eration of Methuselah, all who were high priests, `with the residue of his posterity who were righteous, into the valley of Adam-ondi-Ahman, and there bestowed upon them his last blessing.'[115] At this grand gathering the Lord appeared and administered comfort unto Adam, and said unto him: `I have set thee to be at the head; a multitude of nations shall come of thee, and thou art a prince over them forever.' The assembly arose and blessed Adam, and called him Michael, the prince, the archangel. Then Adam stood up in the midst of the congregation -- and no such gathering on any other occasion has this world ever seen -- `and notwithstanding he was bowed down with age, being full of the Holy Ghost, (he) predicted whatsoever should befall his posterity unto the last generation.' All of this is written in the book of Enoch, which shah be revealed in due time.[116]

"Not many years hence there shall be another gathering of high priests and righteous souls in this same valley of Adam-ondi-Ahman. At this gathering Adam, the Ancient of Days, will again be present. At this time the vision which Daniel saw will be enacted. The Ancient of Days will sit. There will stand before him those who have held the keys of all dispensations, who shall render up their stewardships to the first Patriarch of the race, who holds the keys of salvation. This shall be a Day of Judgment and preparation. Joseph, the Prophet, in speaking of this event, said: `Daniel in his seventh chapter speaks of the Ancient of Days; he means the oldest man, our father Adam, Michael; he will call his children together and hold a council with them to prepare them for the coming of the Son of Man. He (Adam) is the father of the human family, and presides over the spirits of all men, and all that have had the keys must stand before him in this grand council....'[117]

---

115   D&C 107:58
116   D&C 107:54-57
117   History of the Church 3:386-387

"It was in the night vision that all this was shown to Daniel, and he saw the Son of Man come to the grand council, as he did to the first grand council in the valley of Adam-ondi-Ahman, and there he received the keys from Adam `and there was given to him dominion, and glory, and a kingdom, that all people, nations, and languages, should serve him; his dominion is an everlasting dominion, which shall not pass away, and his kingdom that shall not be destroyed.'[118] In this council Christ will take over the reigns of government, officially, on this earth, and `the kingdom and dominion, and the greatness of the kingdom under the whole heaven, shall be given to the people of the Saints of the Most high, whose kingdom is an everlasting kingdom, and all dominions shall serve and obey him,' even Jesus Christ.

"This council in the valley of Adam-ondi-Ahman is to be of the greatest importance to this world. At that time there will be a transfer of authority from the usurper and impostor, Lucifer, to the rightful King, Jesus Christ. Judgment will be set and all who have held keys will make their reports and deliver their stewardships, as they shall be required. Adam will direct this judgment, and then he will make his report, as the one holding the keys for this earth, to his superior officer, Jesus Christ. Our Lord will then assume the reins of government; directions will be given to the Priesthood; and he, whose right it is to rule, will be installed officially by the voice of the Priesthood there assembled. This grand council of Priesthood will be composed, not only of those who are faithful who now dwell on this earth, but also of the prophets and apostles of old, who have had directing authority. Others may also be there, but if so they will be there by appointment, for this is to be an official council called to attend to the most momentous matters concerning the destiny of this earth.

---

118   Daniel 7:18-14

"When this gathering is held, the world will not know of it; the members of the Church at large will not know of it, yet it shall be preparatory to the coming in the clouds of glory of our Savior Jesus Christ as the Prophet Joseph said. The world cannot know of it. The Saints cannot know of it -- except those who officially shall be called into this council -- for it shall precede the coming of Jesus Christ as a thief in the night, unbeknown to all the world."[119]

After the conference at Adam-ondi-Ahman and the formal assumption of government on the earth by the King of Kings, he will appear in the City of the New Jerusalem, and from the temple that is built in his name, will commence a work of utmost importance.

This pre-millennial appearance of the Savior at the New Jerusalem is clearly taught in the scriptures.[120] Under the personal supervision of the Messiah, three projects will then be undertaken. The Lamanite nations will be converted,[121] the Ten Tribes will be brought down from the north,[122] and the righteous blood of Israel will receive a final call to gather out from all other parts of the earth and flee to America.' All these things must be accomplished before the great day of the Lord can come.[123]

The Conversion of the Lamanites

As has been previously pointed out, the conversion of the Lamanites as a whole will occur after they have come into political power.

---

119 Joseph Fielding Smith, The Way to Perfection, chapter 40
120 3 Nephi 20:22; 21:25; D&C 45:66-67; 84:4-5; 97:15-17.
121 3 Nephi 21:26.
122 3 Nephi 21:26.
123 3 Nephi 21:28-29.

Where are the Lamanite nations today?

It is estimated there are over fifty million Indians of pure or mixed blood who are living in South America, Central America and Mexico.[124] The number of Indians living farther north is less than half a million![125] It is not difficult to determine the identity of the nations in which the prophecies of the Lord will be fulfilled.

When these people are converted, they will no longer be backward, mischievous, and unattractive. They will become white like their brethren of Ephraim.[126] They will be highly spiritual, living the commandments of the Lord, and considered by the rest of Israel as a "righteous branch."[127] They will become progressive in their habits, attractive in their demeanor; cultural and intellectual attainment will be theirs. Verily, saith the Lord, they will "blossom as the rose."[128]

---

124   Forester, R.J., U.S. Dept. of Labor pamphlet, 1925. The Racial Problem Involved in Immigration from Latin America"; Encyclopedia Britannica, 14th edition, Vol. 16, p. 503. This estimate of the pure and mixed Indian population is conservative. Officials of the Pan-American Union in Washington, D.C., stated to the writer that South American countries seek to minimize the extent of their Indian population because of the stigma attached to those who are of Indian descent. Officials of the State Department advised the writer that of the 90,000,000 persons living in South America, Central America and Mexico, 75,000,000 are probably of the Indian race.
125   Encyclopedia Britannica, 14th edition, Vol. 16, p. 506.
126   2 Nephi 30:6.
127   2 Nephi 9:53.
128   D&C 49:24.

The Coming of the Ten Tribes from the North

The second great project, and one which will be undertaken contemporaneously with the conversion of the Lamanites, will be the revealing of the whereabouts of the lost Ten Tribes and the gathering of them from the North. This will not be any ordinary event. For over a hundred years, their prophets have been preparing them. As early as 1831 the Lord revealed that the translated Apostle John was fulfilling a mission among the Ten Tribes preparing them for their journey to Zion.[129] When the Lord commands it, and the earth has been prepared for it, the prophets who are among those tribes will "no longer stay themselves,"[130] but will bring multitudes forth.

Where are the Ten Tribes today?

Some students have adopted the views of the Anglo-Israelites, who claim that the countries of northern Europe constitute the tribes of Israel. The word of the Lord on the subject, however, is that they are "separated"[131] and that the main body of them is not among the gentiles at all.[132]

The authorities of the Church confirm this fact. Brigham Young taught that "the Ten Tribes of Israel are on a portion of the earth -- a portion separate from the main land."[133] Joseph Fielding Smith says:

"The Ten Tribes were taken by force out of the land

---

129   Joseph Fielding Smith, Essentials of Church History, p. 126.
130   D&C 133:26.
131   3 Nephi 15:20.
132   3 Nephi 15:15-24.
133   Matthias F. Cowley, Wilford Woodruff, p. 448

the Lord gave them. Many of them mixed with the peoples among whom they were scattered. A large portion, however, departed in one body into the north and disappeared from the rest of the world. Where they went and where they are we do not know. That they are intact we must believe, else how shall the scripture be fulfilled? There are too many prophecies concerning them and their return in a body for us to ignore the fact."[134]

Parley P. Pratt wrote:

"The Jews are called dispersed because they are scattered among the nations; but the Ten Tribes are called outcasts because they are cast out from the knowledge of the nations into a land by themselves."[135]

We may rest assured that the first people on earth to whom this great secret will be finally revealed will be the prophets and chosen Saints of God. They will know the exact location and whereabouts of the lost tribes long before any scientist or society will discover it. "Surely the Lord God will do nothing, but he revealeth his secret unto his servants the prophets."[136]

Regardless of where the Ten Tribes are, it will require a miracle to bring them forth. It will be of greater magnitude than the dividing of the Red Sea in the days of Israel's Exodus. The day is coming when the seed of Jacob will no longer say, "The Lord liveth that brought up the Children of Israel out of the land of Egypt; but the Lord liveth that brought up the Children of Israel out of the North."[137]

Mountains, ice and a continent of water will stand be-

---

134   Joseph Fielding Smith, Way to Perfection, p. 130.
135   Pratt, P. P., Voice of Warning, p. 30.
136   Amos 3:7.
137   Jeremiah 16:14-15.

tween the Ten Tribes and the land of Zion when they first appear, but they will "smite the rocks, and the ice shall flow down at their presence."[138] As they come to the great body of water, dry land will be cast up in the midst of it so that a mighty highway will spread before them.[139] Thus will the God of Jacob fulfill his promise to bring them back to the land of Joseph and crown them with mighty blessings under the hands of the Ephraimite Saints.[140]

Where will the hosts of Israel dwell?

It has been previously pointed out that if the great gentile civilization now inhabiting this land should become unworthy of it, the Lord has warned that he will rid the land of them. Joseph Smith predicted that there would be ample room for the hosts of Israel when they come. He said that the judgments of the Lord "will sweep the wicked of this generation from off the face of the land, to open and prepare the way for the return of the lost tribes of Israel from the North Country."[141] It is apparent that this prophecy is yet to be fulfilled.

It would appear that some of the gentiles who are driven by war and pestilence will seek respite in the northern portion of the continent where they can continue their lives after the design of their own wickedness. Such a people would no doubt resist the migration of the multitudes of Israel as they pour across the great highway. The scriptures plainly speak of the Ten Tribes being confronted by "enemies" who will become their "prey' as they march over them on the way to the capital city of the New Jerusalem."[142]

---

138   D&C 133:26.
139   D&C 133:27; Isaiah 11:16.
140   D&C 133:32.
141   Teachings of Joseph Smith, p 17.
142   D&C 133:28.

And any people, not of Israel, who think they can avail themselves of the great highway and thus flee into the former habitation of the Ten Tribes, will be as surprised and disappointed as the armies of Egypt who attempted to cross dry-shod on the miraculous thoroughfare that opened up suddenly in the midst of the Red Sea. The mighty highway of the latter days will be equally unsafe for the wicked who trespass on it, for Israel alone shall pass over it.[143]

The uniting of the Ten Tribes with the Saints at the New Jerusalem will be glorious indeed, for the hosts of Israel will bring all their records, histories, and scriptures with them.[144]

They will tell of their strange experiences and describe the memorable occasion when the Messiah visited them in the meridian of time.[145]

Furthermore, they will bring with them the treasures of their former habitation -- precious metals, rare gems, and works of art -- all of which will be used, no doubt, to embellish the temple in the city of the New Jerusalem.[146] Then they will receive of the blessings to be had in that sacred edifice, for "there shall they fall down and be crowned with glory, even in Zion, by the hands of the servants of the Lord, even the children of Ephraim."[147]

The Gathering of All the Saints to Zion

Now comes the third important phase of the Lord's work. He is going to call the Saints in the entire world to assemble in Zion. They will not come in haste or as fugitives from persecution, but as Saints of God joyfully returning to

143   Isaiah 35:8-10.
144   2 Nephi 29:12-13.
145   See promise of the Savior in 3 Nephi 15:12-20; 16:1-3.
146   D&C 133:30.
147   D&C 133:32.

the home of their inheritance.[148]

They will come out of all nations as the watchmen on the Mount of Ephraim urge them forward.[149]

And who are the watchmen on the mountain Ephraim? None other than the sons of Ephraim who constitute the officials and the Priesthood holders of the Church and Kingdom of God in the latter days -- to whom all Israel, save Judah alone, will come for their blessings.[150] From among these sons of Ephraim the Lord will select by revelation his special ambassadors who will then receive a dual calling.[151]

First, they must go into the mountains and deserts, the cities and hamlets, among caves and rocks, hunting out the Saints and warning them to gather to America.[152]

Second, they must go into every nation, kindred, tongue and people warning the righteous and repentant to flee to Zion and sealing all those who reject their testimonies unto the day when the arm of the Lord shall fall.[153]

Since the opening of this dispensation, the Lord has been warning his Priesthood that they must perfect themselves in the ministry and prepare for this great mission when they will go in among the gentile nations for the last time, gathering out the Saints and exercising the sealing power of the Priesthood against the remainder who reject them.[154]

If there are any nations in the earth who have not heard

---

148 3 Nephi 21:28-29.
149 Jeremiah 31:6.
150 D&C 133:30-32.
151 D&C 88:84.
152 Jeremiah 16:16; D&C 29:8; Revelation 18:4.
153 D&C 133:71-72.
154 D&C 88:77, 80, 84.

the restored gospel before, they will hear the missionaries explain it at this time. And wherever necessary the gift of tongues will be given to the Elders for the Lord has promised that each nation will hear the gospel preached in his own tongue.[155] They all must have their opportunity before the end can come.[156] Such a calling will tax the missionary system of the Church to the limit, and there will not be any time for the multiplying of words.[157] The missionaries will no doubt proclaim their warning in the highways and market places like the prophets of old, and when they have done all they can in the time allotted they will leave that place -- never again to return.[158]

Thus the multitudes of those who are righteous will flee to the refuge of America and gather as close as they can to the New Jerusalem where the newly converted Lamanites and the great Ten Tribes of Israel will likewise be assembling.[159] The multitudes will be so great we are told that they will make a great noise by reason of their numbers.[160] They will overflow the land, breaking forth on the right hand and on the left, inhabiting the desolated cities left by the gentiles and spreading out over desert and plain.[161]

In that day there will be a great need for water -- both for the thirsty multitudes and the barren land. Concerning that day the scripture says: "I the Lord will hear them, I the God of Israel will not forsake them. I will open rivers in high places, and fountains in the midst of the valleys; I will make the wilderness a pool of water, and the dry land springs of

---

155   D&C 90:11.
156   Matthew 24:14; D&C 133:37.
157   D&C 63:58.
158   See prophecy of Heber C. Kimball; supra p. 27.
159   D&C 29:7-8; 45:66; 115:6.
160   Micah 2:12.
161   3 Nephi 22:3.

water."[162] "Therefore, will I not make solitary places to bud and to blossom, and to bring forth in abundance saith the Lord."[163] "The wilderness and the solitary place shall be glad for them (the gathered children of Israel); and the desert shall rejoice and blossom as the rose."[164]

The Beginning of the End

Lucifer will be perniciously zealous in manifesting his great power among his dominions at that day when the ambassadors of the Lord pass through every kingdom crying repentance.[165] Lucifer's technique will be to feed the sign-seeking multitudes of the earth with sensational exhibitions.[166] He will show them fire coming down from heaven.[167] He will raise up false Christ's and false prophets, and so great will be their powers that even some of the elect will believe.[168]

Lucifer's church will cast its shadow over most of the earth so that outside of Zion all men, small and great, rich and poor, bond and free, will have the identifying mark of that church in their right hand or in their foreheads.[169] No man will be able to buy and sell among them in that day unless he bears that mark in his body.[170]

And what will be the fruits of this satanical institution? Verily, saith the Lord, the nations who give respect to her will reap the all-consuming abomination of desolation

---

162   Isaiah 41:17-18.
163   D&C 117:7.
164   Isaiah 35:1.
165   D&C 1:35.
166   Revelation 16:14.
167   Revelation 13:13-14.
168   Pearl of Great Price, p. 44, v. 22; Matthew 24:11-12.
169   Revelation 13:16.
170   Revelation 13:17.

spoken of by the Prophet Daniel.[171] Nation will rise against nation, kingdom shall rise against kingdom, and in the wake of their war one with another there will come famine and pestilence.[172] In that day it will come to pass that the inhabitants of Zion will be the only people on the face of the earth not subjected to the ravages of war.[173]

In considering the vessels of unrighteousness from which the great modern nations are made drunken, the Lord has said: "For all flesh is corrupted before me; and the powers of darkness prevail upon the earth, among the children of men, in the presence of all the hosts of heaven -- which causeth silence to reign, and all eternity is pained, and the angels are waiting the great command to reap down the earth, to gather the tares that they may be burned; and behold the enemy is combined."[174]

But in that day of which we speak, the period of waiting shall cease. This is the time when the great God of Israel shall commence to reap down the earth. This is the time when those who spurned the warnings of the Elders shall see the patience of the Lord exhausted and the wrath of his indignation sweep down upon all those who have combined together in wickedness. Then "cometh the testimony of earthquakes, which shall cause groanings in the midst of her, and men shall fall upon the ground and shall not be able to stand." Then comes "the testimony of ... thunderings ... of lightnings, and the voice of tempests ... waves of the sea heaving themselves beyond their bounds.... All things shall be in commotion ... surely men's hearts shall fail them; for fear shall come upon all people."[175]

---

171   Matthew 24:15.
172   Pearl of Great Price, p. 44:29.
173   D&C 45:69-70.
174   D&C 38:11-12.
175   D&C 88:89-91.

The earth itself shall begin to stagger in its orbit about the sun.[176] The stars shall be hurled from their place in the firmament and the remainder will not give forth their light.[177] The sun shall suddenly be darkened, and the moon shall be bathed in blood.[178]

Those scholars who doubt the ability of the Lord to literally fulfill these prophecies should learn a lesson from Pharaoh of Egypt who also disbelieved and tempted the Lord to show forth his power. Among other things, this is what we read: "Moses and Aaron did ... as the Lord commanded ... and smote the waters that were in the river, in the sight of Pharaoh, and in the sight of his servants; and all the waters that were in the river were turned to blood. And the fish that was in the river died; and the river stank, and the Egyptians could not drink of the water of the river; and there was blood throughout all the land of Egypt."[179]

America to Be Cut Off From Other Nations

As one contemplates the distress that will exist among mankind in this day, he is led to exclaim: "Will not America then be overrun by multitudes of people fleeing from foreign lands?"

The answer of the Lord is, "No!"

In that day the land of America will be cut off from the rest of the earth by violent seas. "Wherefore the days will come that no flesh shall be safe upon the waters. And it shall be said ... that none is able to go up to the land of Zion upon the waters, but he that is upright in heart."[180]

---

176   D&C 88:87.
177   D&C 34:9.
178   D&C 45:42.
179   Exodus 7:20-21.
180   D&C 61:15-16.

No doubt millions would flee to America during these trying times if the Lord did not make it inaccessible to all except the righteous. This will be the most stringent immigration restriction ever imposed upon this land, and it will be enforced by the violent elements of a treacherous sea.

Parable of the Ten Virgins

During the fast moving events of this day, there will be tens of thousands of latent Latter-day Saints who will suddenly realize that their membership in the Church and Kingdom of the Lord is an enviable possession indeed. And with this realization will come the sudden fear that perhaps they will not be acceptable unto the Lord when he comes.

In the depths of their hearts they will know that they have been slothful, rebellious, critical of the Lord's anointed, refusing to accept missionary calls, neglecting the payment of tithes and offerings. They will know that they have violated their most sacred covenants, desecrated the garment of the Priesthood, and brought disrepute to the Church through adherence to low standards. In short, they will realize that during the years of their laziness, rebellion and indifference they have driven from the temple of their souls the essence of Godliness, the Spirit of the Lord -- the Gift of the Holy Ghost.

This Spirit is the power from beyond the veil which justifies the Saints before their God.[181] And he will be rejected who is found without it at the coming of the Bridegroom, saith the Lord.[182]

This is the source of light, or the oil which the Saints must keep in their lamps, for the Savior says: "And at that day, when I shall come in my glory, shall the parable be

181   Moses 6;60.
182   D&C 45:57; 63:54.

fulfilled which I spake concerning the ten virgins. For they that are wise and have received the truth, and have taken the Holy Spirit for their, guide and have not been deceived -- verily, I say unto you, they shall not be hewn down and cast into the fire, but shall abide the day,"[183] but those who are not prepared at the twelfth hour shall find themselves in the ignoble role the five foolish women.

This parable represents the astonishing fact that half of the Church members will be unworthy and unacceptable when the time for the Second Advent draws near.

The Lord's word concerning them says: "And the foolish said unto the wise, `Give us of your oil; for our lamps are gone out.' But the wise answered, saying, `Not so; lest there be not enough for us and you; but go ye rather to them that sell and buy for yourselves.' And while they went to buy, the bridegroom came; and they that were ready went in with him to the marriage and the door was shut. Afterward came also the other virgins saying, `Lord, Lord, open to us.' But he answered and said, `Verily, I say unto you, I know you not.'"[184]

The Lord's warning in this dispensation is not only to the gentiles, Jews, heathens and Lamanites. It is emphatically proclaimed to the members of the Kingdom. Speaking of our day, the Lord has said:

"I have sworn in my wrath and decreed wars upon the face of the earth, and the wicked shall slay the wicked, and fear shall come upon every nation, and the saints also shall hardly escape.... These things are the things that ye must look for; and, speaking after the manner of the Lord, they are nigh at hand, and in a time to come, even in the day of the coming of the Son of Man.

183   D&C 45:56-57.
184   Matthew 25:8-12.

"And until that hour there will be foolish virgins among the wise; and at that hour cometh an entire separation of the righteous and the wicked; and in that day will I send mine angels to pluck out the wicked and cast them into unquench-able fire."[185]

---

185   D&C 63:33-34, 53:54.

PART III
PROPHECY CONCERNING PALESTINE

The Word of Prophecy on Palestine

We now pause in our consideration of events as they will relate to the American Continent and direct our attention to the important contemporaneous events as they will occur in Europe and Asia.

This is a dispensation in which the Lord has been pleading with the strong, brilliant gentile nations inhabiting those continents. Outside of America they are the great powers of the earth and have control of both the land and the wealth of humanity.

But the time of their opportunity is almost fulfilled. The Lord is grieved by their blind, rebellious and conceited maneuvering by which they frustrate the very blessings which he has designed for them. They boast of their innate superiority over all other peoples, and they have appropriated unto themselves the claim of a "natural and divine right" to subjugate and rule any nation not sufficiently strong to resist them.

They have made the earth's geography into an illogical assortment of bristling armed camps. Students grasp at every straw in the political wind as they attempt to predict from hour to hour what these nations will do with the power they possess.

It is the Lord who knows the truth of the matter. He knows the innermost secrets of the ambitious gentile leaders. He knows their appetite for destruction and aggrandizement, and he knows how they will conspire together to devour the whole earth. Thus it is that the Lord has determined to withdraw his benevolence from them and turn his face toward a weaker and heretofore less-favored people.

This intention of the Lord is one of his great secrets. His

prophets have described it with remarkable detail but since the gentiles have rejected the prophets and the import of their words, the intention of the Lord remains a secret except to a few.

The warning of the Lord is this: Look to Judah!

The ebb and flow of international power in Eurasia is ultimately going to center around the ancient promised land of the Jews. Regardless of the plans and conspiracies of gentile emperors, the climax of their power will come when they march up against this chosen remnant of Judah who will be gathered out from all the earth and prepared against that day when the Lord will reckon with the power of Lucifer as it magnifies itself in the armies of the gentile monarchs. This is the intent of the Lord, and he has told his prophets.

On Washington's Birthday, 1879, Wilford Woodruff addressed himself in the following manner to the children of Judah scattered throughout the world:

"... the Lord has decreed that the Jews should be gathered from all the Gentile nations where they have been driven, into their own land, in fulfillment of the words of Moses their law-giver. And this is the will of your great Elohim, O house of Judah, and whenever you shall be called upon to perform this work, the God of Israel will help you. You have a great future and destiny before you and you cannot avoid fulfilling it; you are the royal chosen seed, and the God of your father's house has kept you distinct as a nation for eighteen hundred years, under all the oppression of the whole Gentile world. You may not wait until you believe on Jesus of Nazareth, but when you meet with Shiloh your king, you will know him; your destiny is marked out, you cannot avoid it.

"It is true that after you return and gather your nation

home, and rebuild your City and Temple, that the Gentiles may gather together their armies to go against you to battle, to take you a prey and to take you as a spoil, which they will do, for the words of your prophets must be fulfilled; but when this affliction comes, the living God that led Moses through the wilderness, will deliver you, and your Shiloh will come and stand in your midst and fight your battles; and you will know him, and the afflictions of the Jews will be at an end, while the destruction of the Gentiles will be so great that it will take the whole house of Israel who are gathered about Jerusalem, seven months to bury the dead of their enemies, and the weapons of war will last them seven years for fuel, so that they need not go to any forest for wood.

"These are tremendous sayings -- who can bear them? Nevertheless they are true and will be fulfilled according to the sayings of Ezekiel, Zechariah and other prophets. Though the heavens and the earth pass away, not one jot or tittle will fall unfulfilled."[186]

The Jewish prophets rejoiced in the coming of this, our day, although, as we shall see, they foresaw it to be an unprecedented era of persecution and suffering for their people. They rejoiced; however, as they saw the raising up of the Jewish Zion and the long awaited arrival of their King Emmanuel. Eventually, they knew their King would come in majesty and power, delivering the besieged city of Jerusalem and reigning over his chosen people in supreme splendor that would attract the fealty of every nation under heaven.

Palestine Is Dedicated

One hundred years ago, the land of Palestine was a home for men and animals of prey. It was the acknowledged graveyard of grandeur long since passed. Its topography was mostly desert with ragged rocks protruding from its

186   Matthias F. Cowley, Wilford Woodruff, pp. 509-510.

hills and mountains. There was nothing glorious about the land, save its history, and thus the prophecies of the ancient revelators were literally fulfilled.[187]

But the prophets rejoiced that in the Lord's own due time this wilderness would be changed into a fruitful land -- a place where the children of Judah could gather together.[188] It was appropriate, therefore, that in this dispensation the Lord should command an official of the Priesthood to go to the land of Palestine and dedicate it for the imminent return of the Jews.

On October 24, 1841, Orson Hyde, a Jewish disciple of the latter day Church, journeyed to the city of old Jerusalem, and from the summit of the Mount of Olives poured from his heart a prayer of dedication unto the Lord.[189]

Subsequently, in the year 1873, George A. Smith was sent by President Brigham Young to again dedicate the land and pray unto the Lord that his work might be hastened unto an opening of the way for the return of the exiled Jews.[190]

The Prodigal Children Returning

In 1917, as one of the products of the First World War, the power and wisdom of the Lord made itself manifest. For the first time in eighteen centuries, the ancient Promised Land finally fell into the hands of a government with a sympathetic understanding of the Jewish problem. And though the territory of Palestine was inhabited by a population of bitterly antagonistic Arabs, it was specifically set apart for a

187   Ezekiel 5; 6:14; Jeremiah 9:9-11.
188   Isaiah 61:4; Ezekiel 36:8-11.
189   Joseph Fielding Smith, Essentials of Church History, p. 284.
190   B. H. Roberts, Comprehensive History of the Church 5:474-475.

Jewish homeland.[191]

Thus began a modern miracle.

Since that time, tired and harassed Jews have turned their vision once again toward old Jerusalem. Those who hesitate are prodded forward by legalized persecution. They are made exiles from lands where their forefathers lived for scores of generations. Their property is confiscated and their lives are threatened. The sudden appearance of anti-Jewish policies in certain foreign nations has hastened the work of the Jewish gathering at a speed which makes a prophecy come true before our very eyes.

Will the Jews Succeed in Palestine?

Nevertheless, there are many students even today who see a multitude of potent forces that may easily thwart the new-born effort to make Palestine a Jewish Home-land. Will the British policy remain favorable in view of the widespread criticism being incited?[192] How can Jewish immigration continue when already thousands of refugees are being turned away for the very real reason that difficulty is being experienced in absorbing them?

The 900,000 native Arabs harbor a vitriolic hatred for the 400,000 Jews now in Palestine. By 1948 the ratio of population in Palestine was estimated to be 1,700,000 Moslem Arabs, 700,000 Jews and 140,000 Christians.[193] This will illustrate how rapidly the land of Palestine is filling up now that residence there has been placed at a premium by both Jews and Arabs. The number of Jews has multiplied twelve times since the end of World War I.[194] The Grand Mufti of Je-

191   H. G. Wells, Outline of History, pp. 1122-1123.
192   L. M. Larson, History of England, 1932, p. 858.
193   See U.S. News and World Report, June 11, 1948.
194   U.S. News and World Report, June 11, 1948.

rusalem, who is President of the Moslem High Council, has threatened the declaration of a general holy war unless the Arabic demands are satisfied. These are uncompromising:

1. Jewish immigration to Palestine must cease immediately.

2. Complete independence and a national government must be granted to the Arabs in Palestine.

3. Great Britain must abandon the idea of a Jewish national home in Palestine, as embodied in the Balfour Declaration.

4. The British Mandate in Palestine must be terminated at once.

5. Further sale of land to Jews in Palestine must be absolutely forbidden by law.

6. Great Britain must conclude a treaty with the Arabs of Palestine, similar to the Anglo-Egyptian, Anglo-Iraqi, and French-Syrian treaties, by which Britain would set up an Arab state in Palestine with full sovereignty and with the Jews having only minority rights.[195]

Authorities point out that the Jews who have assembled in Palestine are not unified in any sense of the word. They speak differently, they believe differently. Their physical characteristics are different.[196]

How can a successful homeland be created for the Jews under such conditions?

---

195 "Holy Terror in Palestine," Current History, December 1938, pp. 24-26.
196 "Tel Aviv, City of the Jews," Reader's Digest, October 1938, p. 60.

To the Latter-day Saints, however, these are not discouraging circumstances. The seeds which have been successfully sown are those out of which will blossom the complete fulfillment of all the words of prophecy given by the Lord. The successful establishment of the Church of Jesus Christ in the latter days occurred under circumstances equally antagonistic. This is the time when a marvelous work and a wonder will be accomplished, and surely the Lord will do it, and the prophecies of economists and statesmen will fail while those of the Lord are vindicated.[197]

In 1879 Wilford Woodruff wrote from the St. George Temple:

"I wish in this testimony to say that the time is not far distant when the rich men among the Jews will be called upon to use their abundant wealth to gather the dispersed of Judah, and purchase the ancient dwelling places of their fathers in and about Jerusalem, and rebuild the holy city and temple."[198]

The extent to which this prophecy has already been fulfilled may best be appreciated by considering the fact that American Jews alone have contributed over $200,000,000 for the rebuilding of Jerusalem.[199]

Standing firmly behind the British mandate in Palestine is the United States Government. As a result of the Anglo-American convention in 1924, it has the right to object to any change of policy by Britain toward Palestine.

---

197   D&C 101:10, 19; 29:10, 21; 3 Nephi 29:2-3.
198   Matthias F. Cowley, Wilford Woodruff, p. 509.
199   "Holy Terror in Palestine," Current History, December 1938, p. 26. This was the total amount as of December, 1938. However, by 1948 this sum had mounted to $700,000,000. See U.S. News and World Report, June 11, 1948.

Under date of October 22, 1938, "President Roosevelt let it be known that he and the government at Washington are `for the maintenance of Palestine as a Jewish national home without limitation.' Moreover, ignoring the prospect of world-wide pan-Arab revolt, it was indicated that `everything within the power of the United States Government would be done to prevent the curtailment of Jewish immigration into Palestine'."[200]

This vigorous policy has continued. The United States led the fight for a Jewish homeland following World War II and as a result the Jews in Palestine were permitted to set up an independent state of Israel on May 15, 1948. It was on this date that the British terminated their supervisory government of Palestine which they received under mandate from the League of Nations after World War I and from the United Nations after World War II. The new state of Israel was immediately recognized by the United States.[201]

And now, hear the word of the Lord on the matter: "And they shall build the old wastes, they shall raise up the former desolations, and they shall repair the waste cities, the desolations of many generations."[202] "And I will bring again the captivity of my people Israel, and they shall build the waste cities, and inhabit them; and they shall plant vineyards, and drink the wine thereof; they shall also make gardens, and eat the fruit of them."[203]

Thus the Jews will build flourishing cities throughout their ancient promised land and surround themselves with culture and wealth. Once again Jerusalem shall become mighty unto her people.[204] There will be a great temple

200   U.S. News and World Report, June 11, 1948.
201   U.S. News and World Report, June 11, 1948.
202   Isaiah 61:4.
203   Amos 9:14.
204   3 Nephi 20:29-34.

erected within her walls.[205] During this time they will feel so secure in their new golden age, which they will not even bother to prepare defenses against possible enemies.[206] Their cities will not be protected, neither will they raise up armies unto themselves. Then, as has always been the case in past history, the growth and accumulated prosperity of the Jews will become the envy of surrounding Gentile nations.[207]

Preparing for the Last World War before the Millennium

In our day there are wars and rumors of wars, and no man can predict from year to year which nation will survive in the struggle. Boundaries are being changed, trodden over, and broken down. Law is not granted its usual degree of respect either within nations or among them. The jungle jargon of "might makes right" is regaining its former favor among the rulers of men.

These exact circumstances were predicted by Wilford Woodruff.[208]

And with the breakdown of domestic and international law there has followed a spirit of war and conquest which is being whipped into a tempest by the leaders of powerful nations. Once this spirit begins to operate, it will not be turned back, Brigham Young says. It will go through them.[209]

This means that regardless of who wins the present gigantic struggles in war, intolerance is going to continue to grow, anti-Semitism will continue to grow. The spirit of war and conquest is going to increase. The greed of nations will

---

205   Revelation 11:1-2.
206   Ezekiel 38:11.
207   Ezekiel 38:14.
208   Matthias F. Cowley, Wilford Woodruff, p. 511.
209   Discourses of Brigham Young, p. 561.

not be satisfied. This is the day when Lucifer is given power to magnify himself in all his satanical glory among the nations who seek to serve him.[210]

How Will It End?

Ezekiel addressed a prophecy to the nation that is ultimately going to dominate the power politics of Europe and Asia.[211]

It is going to be an exceedingly powerful nation, satiated with greed and aggrandizement. All other nations will be combined under it and its leader is referred to by Ezekiel as "Gog, Chief Prince of Meshech and Tubal." Under him will also be the people of Magog, Gomer and Togarmah. All these are descendants of Japheth, father of the Gentiles.[212]

The meaning of Ezekiel is clear: A single gentile nation is going to eventually encompass all other gentile nations of Asia and Europe so that they will form one large company together. And at the head of this federation of militant nations will stand a dominating prince of Japheth, an uncompromising, ruthless, gentile dictator.

Daniel saw this nation and this leader. He described the nation as "dreadful, terrible, and strong exceedingly."[213] He said it should "be diverse from all other kingdoms;" that it would "devour the whole earth, and ... tread it down and break it in pieces."[214] He saw the man whom Ezekiel addressed as "Gog." Daniel said he would be different from all other rulers on the earth and that he would "speak great words against the Most High ... wear out the Saints of the

---

210   D&C 1:35.
211   Ezekiel, chapters 38 and 39.
212   Genesis 10:2-3.
213   Daniel 7:7.
214   Daniel 7:23.

Most High and think to change times and laws."[215]

Who is Gog?

In Ezekiel's day, one of the strong gentile nations in the earth was Magog, or the Scythians, as they were called by the Greeks.[216] And their king was called Gog.[217] The name "Gog" is obviously used in a representative sense by Ezekiel just as he uses the names of Japheth's children to represent the gentile nations under Gog. In the Book of Revelation the Apostle John likewise uses the names "Gog" and "Magog" to represent the rebellious gentiles. It should be noted, however, that John is referring to the gentiles and their leader who will rise up toward the end of the Millennium.[218] This gentile uprising spoken of by John must not be confused with the pre-Millennial uprising of "Gog" and "Magog" referred to by Ezekiel and Daniel.

We do not hasten to identify any contemporary nation or personality with these prophecies. We simply affirm that when history is written, no man will find difficulty in ascertaining the identity of the nation and the man to whom Ezekiel, Daniel and their fellow prophets had reference. Already the spirit and policies which are to characterize Gog and his nation are being manifested in several great gentile peoples. The particular nation which will ultimately assume the self-appointed role of supremacy yet remains for the future to reveal. When it clearly appears, however, we shall behold its commander-in-chief and know that he is Gog.

Gog will overcome all those who resist him until he will head a great company of heavily armed nations. It will be in that day that every man who refuses to take up his

215   Daniel 7:24-25.
216   Cambridge Companion to the Bible, under "Magog."
217   Cambridge Companion to the Bible, under "Gog."
218   Revelation 20:7-8.

sword and fight must necessarily flee to the American Continent.[219] And it will be in that day that the strife among the gentiles and heathens will be so wide-spread that America, alone, will be free from war.[220] Thus will the earth be overshadowed by the abomination of desolation spoken of by Daniel,[221] and referred to by the Messiah while he was teaching his disciples in Jerusalem.[222]

Palestine, an Object of Conquest

Who among men save the prophets of the Lord would anticipate that the comparatively insignificant territory of Palestine could ultimately become the apex of a world-wide struggle. After Gog has at last absorbed all other gentile nations, the Prophet Ezekiel predicts that he will turn his greedy war machine on the prosperous land of Palestine. He will say:

"I will go up to the land of unwalled villages; I will go to them that are at rest, that dwell safely, all of them dwelling without walls, and having neither bars nor gates, to take spoil, and to take a prey; to turn thine (my) hand upon the desolate places that are now inhabited, and on the people that are gathered out of the nations, which have gotten cattle and goods, that shall dwell in the midst of the land."[223]

And the Lord declares: "Thou shalt come up against my people of Israel, as a cloud to cover the land; it shall be in the latter days, and I will bring thee against my land ... O Gog...."[224]

---

219   D&C 45:68.
220   D&C 45:69.
221   Daniel 9:27.
222   Joseph Smith - Matthew, verses 31, 32, 34.
223   Ezekiel 38:11-12.
224   Ezekiel 38:16.

Thus will the gentiles undertake the greatest military campaign of which we have any record, and they will go forth by the power of Lucifer to completely overwhelm the children of Judah.

The March on Jerusalem

John the Beloved saw this great event when the highly mechanized armies of all nations would be on the march.[225] He saw the hordes of combatants riding on their self-propelled vehicles of death. Ezekiel describes them as a cloud covering the land, but John was told the number of their ranks. They totaled 200,000,000![226]

Consider the desolation that will follow such an army, or even a fraction of such an army, as it charges into the unprotected Holy Land the Jews.

We do not read of any resistance being made by the Jews until the gentile armies finally reach the walls of the capital city, Jerusalem. Apparently the outlying "unfenced" cities will fall before the thundering war machine of Gog without daring to protest. But at Jerusalem the Jews will make their stand, and a comparatively successful resistance will be made. The gentile hosts will batter at the besieged Jews and trod down a great portion of their city, but they will not have power to destroy the people as a whole. For three and a half years the Jews will continue to survive the onslaughts Gog.[227]

---

225 Revelation, Chapter 11.
226 Revelation 9:16. John calls these warriors "horsemen," but note his description of the objects on which they were mounted.
227 Daniel 7:25; Revelation 11:2.

A Miracle among the Jews

How will the Jews escape? How will the overwhelming forces of Gog be held at bay three and a half years? Behold, said the prophets, the Lord will do it. It will be during the siege of Gog on Jerusalem that the Lord will begin to make bare his holy arm on behalf his people. He will raise up among the Jews two mighty prophets. Then, as the hosts Gog sweep in against Jerusalem, these two prophets will stand forth to resist them. No military power which the Jews will then have could do it, but the Lord will do it. The all-consuming war machine of Gog will meet an unexpected source of opposition as it marches on the world capital of Judah.

Speaking of these two Jewish witnesses and their resistance to the overwhelming evil their day, an angel declared unto John:

"If any man will hurt them, fire proceedeth out of their mouth, and devoureth their enemies; and if any man will hurt them, he must in this manner be killed. These have power to shut heaven that it rain not in the days of their prophecy; and have power over waters to turn them to blood and to smite the earth with all plagues, as often as they will."[228]

Thus will these two chosen servants of God let fly the first shafts of the Lord's indignation upon the greedy gentile hosts of Gog. They will hold the armies back by the showing forth of mighty miracles while they seal up their testimonies and declare to the Jews that the Messiah will save them if they but endure this hour of travail.

---

228   Revelation 11:5-6.

The Beginning of the End in Jerusalem

And even as these prophets call upon the Lord to reveal his power, so shall it come to pass. The nations living in that day shall see the beginning of the reaping formerly referred to in connection with the events as they are to occur in the land of America.

This is the day when the convulsions of the earth, the overflowing of the seas, and the troubled frenzy of the heaven's constellations will testify to all nations that the cup of the Lord's indignation is filled to its full level. In three brief years the earth will pass through events that will cause men's hearts to fail them, and fear shall come upon all people.[229] This is the day when a portion of the Lord's power will scourge the earth before the end comes.

But Gog, in his stubborn fury will yet rage against Jerusalem, and in a final surge of diabolical strength he and his fighting hosts will succeed in killing the two great prophets of the Jews.[230] It will be when they have finished their testimony.[231] With a triumphant glee the gentile monarch will spread abroad the news of their death. Their bodies will lie in the streets of Jerusalem and Gog will not permit them to be buried. There these bodies will remain for three days and a half while "they that dwell upon the earth shall rejoice over them, and make merry, and shall send gifts one to another because these two prophets tormented them that dwelt on the earth."[232]

With the death of these prophets, no doubt the words of Zechariah will then be fulfilled, for he said: "The city shall be taken, and the houses rifled and the women ravished; and

229   D&C 88:91.
230   Revelation 11:7.
231   Revelation 11:7.
232   Revelation 11:10.

half of the city shall go forth into captivity...."[233]

But at the end of three and a half days, even as Gog is about to triumph over the stricken city at last, a miracle will occur. To the astonishment of them all, the bodies of the two Jewish prophets lying in the streets shall suddenly be quickened and great fear shall come upon the people as they see them rise upon their feet. Then a great voice will be heard from heaven saying: "Come up hither," and the two prophets will ascend in a cloud even as their enemies behold them.[234]

For Gog and his army, this is the end of the world. In an instant they shall see the glory of the Second Coming of the Son of Man.

The Second Coming as Gog Will See It

No imagination can conceive the amazement that will sweep over all men as the Lord suddenly rolls away the veil which separates our mortal earth from the cosmos of eternity that surrounds it.[235]

The Great Emmanuel will suddenly appear and be seen by all people together in a revelation of glory surpassing description. At that moment he will launch the cleansing and quickening of this planet as the prophets predicted, and Gog and his hosts will find themselves bound into bundles ready to be burned. The immeasurable terror which will strike their hearts is best understood when we consider the cataclysmic avalanche of events through which they will pass.

As the Lord appears he shall "utter his voice, and all

---

233   Zechariah 14:2.
234   Revelation 11:11-12.
235   D&C 101:23.

the ends of the earth shall hear it."[236] Immediately, a great earthquake shall roar through the earth with a violence that has never before been known.[237] "The Mountains shall be thrown down, and the steep places shall fall, and every wall shall fall to the ground."[238] The fury of the Lord shall come upon the great ships that traffic in the seas,[239] and also upon the mighty cities, "upon every high tower and every fenced wall."[240] We read that "before the day of the Lord ... the sun shall be darkened, and the moon be turned into blood, and the stars fall from heaven,"[241] and at the coming of the Lord these signs shall continue, together with a multitude of others. For we read: "And so great shall be the glory of his presence that the sun shall hide his face in shame and the moon shall withhold its light, and the stars shall be hurled from their places."[242] "He shall command the great deep, and it shall be driven back into the north countries, and the islands shall become one land."[243] "And there shall be earthquakes also in divers places, and many desolations."[244]

While these great changes are taking place in the earth, the wrath of the Lord will be poured out upon Gog and his multitudes. In addition to the earthquake there will be a flood of water[245] and a great hailstorm mixed with fire.[246] John saw the hail stones that they were about the weight of a talent, and he said that men would blaspheme because of

236   D&C 45:49.
237   Revelation 16:18.
238   Ezekiel 38:20.
239   2 Nephi 12:16; Isaiah 2:16.
240   2 Nephi 12:15.
241   D&C 45:42.
242   D&C 133:49.
243   D&C 133:23.
244   D&C 45:33.
245   Ezekiel 38:22.
246   Ezekiel 38:22; Revelation 8:7.

the plague of this hail.[247] A desolating sickness will cover the land.[248] "And this shall be the plague wherewith the Lord will smite all the people who have fought against Jerusalem: Their flesh shall consume away while they stand upon their feet, and their eyes shall consume away in their holes, and their tongue shall consume away in their mouth.[249] And it shall come to pass in that day that a great tumult from the Lord shall be among them; and they shall lay hold everyone on the hand of his neighbor."[250]

"Every man's sword shall be against his brother;"[251] "... and the wicked shall slay the wicked and fear shall come upon every man."[252]

The warmongering merchantmen of that day shall behold the upheaval all around them and leave their treasures for the moles and the bats while they flee "into the clefts of the rocks and into the tops of the ragged rocks, for the fear of the Lord shall come upon them...."[253]

John, describing the scene, said: "And the kings of the earth, and the great men, and the rich men, and the chief captains and the mighty men, and every bondman, and every free man, hid themselves in the dens and in the rocks of the mountains; and said to the mountains and rocks, Fall on us, and hide us from the face him that sitteth on the throne and from the wrath of the Lamb; for the great day of wrath is come, and who shall be able to stand?"[254]

---

247   Revelation 16:21.
248   D&C 45:32.
249   Zechariah 14:12; D&C 29:19-20.
250   Zechariah 14:13.
251   Ezekiel 38:21.
252   D&C 63:33.
253   2 Nephi 12:20-21.
254   Revelation 6:14-17; Hosea 10:8.

The ships and the harbors, the factories and skyscrapers; the millers and merchantmen, the makers of music and all those who have helped the wicked on the earth to live "deliciously," shall see their handiwork a desolation.[255] And the few gentiles who survive the cleansing of the earth shall behold the destruction of all that they had considered most precious and will weep and wail for "in an hour is she made desolate."[256]

Many students today believe that the cleansing of the earth by fire is a characteristic only of the earth's refining at the end of the Millennium. But there shall likewise be a consuming conflagration at the particular time of which we are now speaking as witness the reference of the Lord to the Second Coming: "... the earth shall pass away so as by fire."[257] "And every corruptible thing, both of man, or of the beasts of the field, or of the fowls of the heavens, or of the fish of the sea, that dwells upon all the face of the earth, shall be consumed; and also that of element shall melt with fervent heat; and all things shall become new, that my knowledge and glory may dwell upon all the earth."[258] Isaiah also plainly declares: "Therefore hath the curse devoured the earth, and they that dwell therein are desolate; therefore the inhabitants of the earth are burned, and few men left."[259]

Surely, as Daniel predicted, "this is the end of the matter,"[260] particularly for Gog and the many nations with him. We are told that out of all their multitudes of mighty warriors, together with their wives and children, there will be but one-sixth left.[261] As for the heathens of that day, they

255 Revelation, Chapter 18.
256 Revelation 18:19.
257 D&C 43:32.
258 D&C 101:24-25.
259 Isaiah 24:6.
260 Daniel 7:28.
261 Ezekiel 39:1-2.

will be dealt with more tolerably, for the Lord will set his glory among them and they shall see his judgment.[262] A few gentile nations will survive, but their dominions will all be taken away.[263] Thus will the earth be prepared for a reign of righteousness by him whose right it is to reign, and a government will be established among every people in the earth, patterned after the holy order of heaven.[264]

Second Coming Seen From a Different Point of View by the Saints

It will be the beloved of God who are called to be Saints who will be given the authority of government over the nations of the earth after the Millennium is established.[265] These are the Saints whom the great Messiah will bring with him when he appears in the clouds of heaven.[266]

Prior to this time, however, the Saints will have passed through a period of extensive preparation. As previously stated, the Savior will appear in the midst of the Saints long before he shows himself to the rest of the world, and a great work will be accomplished under his direct supervision during the very time that Gog and the gentile nations are preparing for war and living recklessly in Europe and Asia.

Therefore, the view which the Saints will have of the Second Coming will be far different from that of the heedless gentiles. The building of the New Jerusalem, the gathering of the Ten Tribes, the conversion of the Lamanites, and the last great missionary call to the nations of the earth are all preliminary steps which the Lord will require at the hands of

262   Ezekiel 39:21.
263   Daniel 7:12.
264   D&C 133:25; 38:21.
265   Joseph Fielding Smith, Way to Perfection, p. 313 and Revelation 20:6.
266   D&C 76:62-64.

the Saints before the end can come.[267]

In addition to the organizing of the Priesthood on the earth, the angelic hosts beyond the veil are to have a great task to perform. From the scriptures we know that they are charged with the reaping down of the earth -- the burning of the tares, the resurrecting of the dead, and the gathering of Israel.[268]

But already the Lord's kingdom beyond the veil is ready to perform its part of the work. In the year 1832, the Lord declared: "Behold ... the angels are crying unto the Lord day and night, who are ready and waiting to be sent forth to reap down the fields."[269] Thus, we see that the angels, though they know neither the day nor the hour of their call,[270] are ready and waiting to perform their great mission.

The Sealing of the 144,000

Just prior to the commencement of the final tribulations on the earth, we are told of an important event which will transpire among the Saints. From among the tribes of Israel the Lord will select 144,000 special ambassadors.[271] These will be chosen and sealed up under the direction of the Apostle John.[272]

12,000 will be gathered from out of each tribe,[273] and their special calling is going to be to preach the gospel to the heathen and gentile people who survive the cleansing

---

267   See "Prophecy Concerning America" above.
268   D&C 63:54; Teachings of the Prophet Joseph Smith, pp. 231-232, 100-101.
269   D&C 86:5; 38:12.
270   D&C 49:7.
271   D&C 133:18; 77:11; Revelation 14:1.
272   D&C 77:14.
273   Revelation 7:4.

of the earth.[274] The work of selecting this group of 144,000 High Priests and sealing them up unto Elohim, the Father, will be an arduous undertaking. John tells us that it will be necessary to hold back the angels who are to reap down the earth until this work can be accomplished.[275] And when it is finished, the preliminary scourges of the Lord previously mentioned will sweep the earth as a testimony to all nations who rejected the missionaries when they made their final call to them.

The Sign of the Coming of the Son of Man

Then the Lord will show forth a great sign which will be a signal to the Saints that the curtain of the Lord's veil is about to be raised on the opening scenes of the Millennium.[276]

Speaking of this sign, the Prophet Joseph said: "Then will appear one grand sign of the Son of Man in heaven. But what will the world do? They will say it is a planet, a comet, etc. But the Son of Man will come (even) as the sign of the coming of the Son of Man, which will be as the light of the morning cometh out of the east."[277]

So the earth will be made ready, and an angel will declare that the wicked are bound together to receive the consuming judgment of the Lord. The righteous will have been gathered from among the tares and the field will be ready to be burned.[278]

Then there will be silence in heaven for the space of half

---

274   D&C 77:11.
275   Revelation 7:3.
276   D&C 88:93; Matthew 24:30.
277   Teachings of the Prophet Joseph Smith, p. 287.
278   D&C 88:94.

an hour.[279] All things will no doubt have been prepared, and this is the moment of quiet waiting just before the showing forth of the face of the Lord and his concourse of heavenly hosts to the agnostic inhabitants of the earth.

Suddenly there will be a great earthquake,[280] and immediately "… shall the curtain of heaven be unfolded, as a scroll is unfolded after it is rolled up, and the face of the Lord shall be unveiled."[281] Thus will the spiritual environment which surrounds the earth be made visible to all the world, and in an instant the Saints who are dwelling upon the earth shall be quickened and caught up to meet the Great Emmanuel.[282]

This is the coming of the Bridegroom at the midnight hour referred to in the parable of the ten virgins, when only half of the Church and Kingdom will be prepared to meet him,[283] and those who have slept and did not look forth for the day of his coming but said he had postponed it[284] shall weep and wail, for verily, they shall not abide the day.[285]

But the Saints who have labored with their might to build the Kingdom will in this hour be translated and caught up to meet the Great Jehovah as he shall appear in the clouds of heaven.[286]

This is the moment when there will be a complete dividing of the righteous from the wicked so that "two shall be in the field; the one shall be taken, and the other left. Two shall be grinding at the mill; the one shall be taken, and the other

---

279 D&C 88:95; Revelation 8:1.
280 D&C 88:89; 43:18.
281 D&C 88:95.
282 D&C 88:96.
283 D&C 45:56.
284 D&C 45:26.
285 D&C 45:44.
286 D&C 88:96.

left."[287]

The Resurrection of the Dead

And even as the Saints are caught up, Michael the Archangel, known to us as Father Adam,[288] will stand forth holding the keys of resurrection and he and the members of the Priesthood who will have been previously organized beyond the veil for this purpose, will call from the graves of the dead the bodies of all those who have a right to be resurrected at this time.[289] They will come forth in glorious rejoicing, every man with his kindred and be caught up into heaven to join the Savior and his Saints. There they will be shown forth in glory before the eyes of all the people on the earth.[290]

The Second Coming As It Will Appear to the Jews

This mighty revelation of the Lord surrounded by a vanguard of 144,000 High Priests and a numberless host of Saints and prophets will literally fulfill the expectation of the Jews who will see their salvation in an hour when they sorely need it. For the event of the Second Coming will occur just as Gog and his armies are about to overwhelm the stricken city of Jerusalem, and the appearance of the Messiah will save the children of Judah from utter destruction.[291]

According to the prophets, the Lord will descend with his hosts to the Mount of Olives,[292] and as the Savior stands

---

287   Joseph Smith - Matthew, verses 44 and 45; Matthew 24:40
288   D&C 27:11.
289   D&C 29:26; Brigham Young's Discourses, p. 571; D&C 78:16.
290   D&C 88:97.
291   Zechariah 12:9.
292   Revelation 14:1; Zechariah 14:4-5; D&C 133:20.

upon it, that prominence will split asunder so as to make a huge valley through which the inhabitants of Jerusalem can flee.[293] Then the wrath of the Lord will be poured out upon the blasphemous Gog and his nations, and the bodies of their dead shall cover all the land.[294]

The light of day will continue through the night time, and though it will not be bright, it will nevertheless be light.[295]

As the Jews escape into the security which the Lord will make for them, they will gather about their Messiah even as did the Nephites of old, and shall glory in his presence. But even as they shall come close unto him, they will beseech him, saying, "What are these wounds in thine hands and in thy feet?" Then he will say "These wounds are the wounds with which I was wounded in the house of my friends...."[296]

Suddenly the Jews will come to know the true identity of their Messiah, and they will be stunned by the realization. "And they shall look upon me (him) whom they have pierced, and they shall mourn for him as one mourneth for his only son.... In that day shall there be a great mourning in Jerusalem ... and the land shall mourn, every family apart."[297] Thus will that generation of Jews mourn for the folly of their bigoted and rebellious fathers who crucified their Messiah in the meridian of time.

The Destiny of Judah

And when the period of mourning is over, there will be a great work for the children of Judah. Their land must be

293   Zechariah 14:4-5; D&C 45:48.
294   Ezekiel 39:1-8.
295   Zechariah 14:6-7.
296   D&C 45:51-53.
297   Zechariah 12:10-12.

cleansed from the carnage of war.[298] Their holy city of Jerusalem must be restored.[299] They must prepare themselves for the distinction and honor which will flow unto them from their King of Righteousness who will be the ruler of all the earth.[300]

The Prophet Ezekiel tells us that it will take the Jews seven months to cleanse the land of its dead.[301] The fallen hosts of Gog will all be buried together in a mighty valley which will be called "Hamon-gog," meaning "the multitude of Gog."[302] And the Jews will be made rich with the treasures and spoils which will be left by those multitudes of Gog who had intended to despoil Judah.[303] The accumulated weapons, supplies, and equipment left by the army of Gog will supply the Jews with sufficient fuel to last seven years.[304]

And when their great labor is completed, the city of Jerusalem will become a world capital, sharing its honor with the city of Zion or the New Jerusalem.[305] The Jewish people will be greatly sought after. The heathens shall know that they are a people sanctified unto the Lord,[306] "and it shall come to pass, that every one that is left of all the nations which came against Jerusalem shall even go up from year to year to worship the King, the Lord of Hosts, and to keep the feast of tabernacles."[307]

---

298   Ezekiel 39:14-16.
299   Ezekiel 36:33; Teachings of the Prophet Joseph Smith, p. 286.
300   Zechariah 14:9; D&C 133:25.
301   Ezekiel 39:12.
302   Ezekiel 39:11.
303   Ezekiel 39:10.
304   Ezekiel 39:9.
305   Joseph Fielding Smith, Way to Perfection, p. 312
306   Ezekiel 37:28.
307   Zechariah 14:16.

Let the children of Judah who now suffer persecution be comforted, for their persecutors will come to them in the day of the Lord to seek salvation from their hands, "yea, many people and strong nations shall come to seek the Lord of hosts in Jerusalem, and to pray before the Lord.... In those days it shall come to pass that ten men shall take hold out of all languages of the nations, even shall take hold of the skirt of him that is a Jew, saying, we will go with you, for we have heard that God is with you."[308]

---

308   Zechariah 8:22-23.

PART IV
PROPHECY CONCERNING
THE MILLENNIUM

The Millennium

In the heartbeat of the soul of every human being there lies a relative degree of passion for perfection. It is the Platonic dream of beauty in the ultimate, of truth in the absolute and of nature in Utopia. These aspirations of the human intellect are perpetually endowed with the hope that sometime, somehow, a perfect order of heaven on earth will be established wherein all things will work together in a symphonic harmony forever.

In sixty centuries of man-made history the lineal descendants of Adam and Eve have struggled toward this destiny.

That there shall be such an era, the Lord assures us: "The great Millennium of which I have spoken by the mouth of my servants shall come."[309] And then he declared: "Let the solemnities of eternity rest upon your minds," and "gird up your loins lest ye be found among the wicked. Lift up your voices and spare not. Call upon the nations to repent, both old and young, both bond and free, saying: Prepare yourselves for the great day of the Lord."[310]

The Millennium -- A Necessary Part of the Plan of Salvation

The discussion of pre-Millennial events covered in the first two sections of this work might raise pertinent inquiries: "Why must the apocalyptic scourges of disease, famine, pestilence, floods, hail, earthquake, wars and finally a conflagration of the very elements themselves, sweep the rebellious inhabitants of the earth involuntarily back into the spirit world from whence they came? Why must the whole earth be changed -- the seas driven back, all lands made into

---

309   D&C 43:30.
310   D&C 43:19-20.

one and every mountain laid low? Why must modern cities become a desolation and kingdoms be torn asunder?"

From the word of the Lord we learn that it is to prepare the earth for the end of the Second Estate. The winding up scenes men in mortality are upon us.

The whole human race must be sifted, sorted and assigned their separate stations. The atonement of Jesus Christ would be of no avail whatever and the earth would be utterly wasted in the end if all the loose threads of six thousand years of human life upon the earth were not grafted together and bound up.[311]

Every person, whether living or dead, must have an opportunity to hear and accept or reject the gospel. Sealing ordinances must be performed. Endowments must be given. The patriarchal pattern of family unity must be extended to every person worthy of the Celestial Kingdom. And an accounting must be made of every soul that has ever been born. Every human being must be motivated in seeking some degree of glory and exaltation. The only ones excluded will be the sons of perdition whose crimes have circumvented the provisions of the plan of salvation. For all the rest of those who have passed through mortality, the Millennium will provide a thousand years of repentance, instruction and reconciliation; a time in which to prepare the entire human race for its ultimate presentation to the Heavenly Father by his Son, Jesus Christ.[312]

An Important Work Reserved for the Millennium

The task of unifying and preparing the human family

311   D&C 2:1-3; Teachings of the Prophet Joseph Smith, p. 337-338.
312   1 Corinthians 15:24; D&C 76:106-107.

for eternity will be a tremendous undertaking. Consider the chasms which separate nations and individuals whether living or dead.

Since the days of Abel, the strong have robbed, ravaged and killed. They have plundered the poor and pillaged the weak. Think of the passion for vengeance which exists in the breasts of the wronged -- those who have been cheated of happiness, of their earthly possessions, who have had their lives shortened or scarred by the indecencies of powerful, grasping fellow beings. These will have demands to make upon justice-pressing punishment to the uttermost farthing.

Who will teach charity and forgiveness to such of these? Who will secure the balm of forgiveness from the wounded and the ravished to blend with the sorrow and repentance of the guilty? In these queries we behold the titanic task of Godhood -- to bring to pass repentance and forgiveness among all nations, creeds and peoples, to ultimately achieve an actual, literal brotherhood of man and prepare the whole human race for the great final judgment. This is the work of the Millennium.

The Surface of the Earth to be Changed

In order to perform the work of the Millennium in the allotted time, many remarkable changes will be inaugurated. The physical improvement of the earth itself will be one of the changes.

At present nearly three-fourths of the earth's surface is submerged under water. The remainder is broken up into fragments of land -- islands and irregular continents -- washed by vast, restless seas and corrugated with perpendicular mountain ranges, broad desolate deserts and deep lethal morasses of swampland.

All this must make way for the Millennium. In that awe-inspiring moment of convulsion and conflagration which will accompany the appearance of the Lord on the Mount of Olives, "He shall command the great deep, and it shall be driven back into the north countries, and the islands shall become one land."[313] John the Revelator described it as a great earthquake "such as was not since men were upon the earth,"[314] and he said: "Every mountain and island were moved out of their places."[315] Referring to the same thing, Isaiah said: "Every valley shall be exalted and every mountain and hill shall be made low; and the crooked shall be made straight and the rough places plain."[316] The snow-capped peaks of mountain chains will crash from their pinnacles in the sky and the deep valleys of desert and marshlands will fill themselves with the debris.

These terrestrial convulsions will be every whit as terrible as the upheaval on the American continent incident to the death of Christ. On that occasion the sinking of mountains, the raising of valleys, the splitting asunder of the seams in the earth sent up such a curtain of volcanic dust and smoke that the whole face of the land was dark for three days. "The inhabitants thereof who had not fallen could feel the vapor of darkness. And there could be no light, because of the darkness, neither candles, neither torches.... And there was not any light seen, neither fire, nor glimmer, neither the sun, nor the moon, nor the stars, for so great were the mists of darkness which were upon the face of the land."[317]

The description of this past event gives literal significance to Jeremiah's prophetic account of that future event when not only this continent but the crust of the whole earth

313   D&C 133:23-24.
314   Revelation 16:18.
315   Revelation 6:12-14.
316   Isaiah 40:4.
317   3 Nephi 8:20-22.

will roll and quake: "I beheld the earth, and lo, it was without form and void; and the heavens, and they had no light. I beheld the mountains, and lo they trembled, and all the hills moved lightly.... I beheld and lo, the fruitful place was a wilderness, and all the cities thereof were broken down at the presence of the Lord."[318]

John the Revelator also said: "Lo, there was a great earthquake, and the sun became black as sackcloth of hair."[319]

All of this elemental debacle is designed but for one purpose -- to restore the earth to its former perfection. The result will be the replacement of nature's hostile barriers with the graceful contour of broad meadows and rich plains, broken only by shallow vales or gentle slopes and extending to the rim of the horizon in every direction.[320]

The Earth to Become As It Was Before It Was Divided

Four generations after the Great Flood, the earth was "divided." It would appear that this event, which took place in the days of Peleg, was caused by the sinking of certain portions of the earth's surface thereby permitting vast regions to be flooded by the sea. No longer was man's habitation "one land" but it was divided into islands and continents and America thereby lost its former connection with the mainland of Eurasia.

Today only 28% of the earth's surface is above sea level[321] and since much of the terrain is difficult to cultivate, the present population potential of the earth is greatly restricted. This will be changed.

---

318   Jeremiah 4:23-26.
319   Revelation 6:12.
320   Luke 3:5.
321   Encyclopedia Americana, 1946 edition, Vol. 12, p. 425.

Not only will the existing terrain become smooth and productive,[322] but "the great deep ... shall be driven back into the north countries and the islands shall become one land ... and the earth shall be like as it was in the days before it was divided."[323]

The reclamation of the ocean floor by the rolling back of the sea and the leveling of the continental plateaus to the mean land-level of the earth will obviously result in multiplying the available surface of the earth many times. And by joining the land into one continent the problems of commerce and communication will be greatly minimized.

Concerning the "Sea East"

Although the land will apparently be joined into one global continent, it does not necessarily mean that it will form a band extending completely around the equatorial circumference of the earth. It appears from the writings of the ancient patriarchs that there was always a channel of sea in the region of our present Atlantic Ocean which probably connected the Arctic and Antarctic Oceans. This conclusion is drawn from the fact that in the days of Enoch (which was before the "division") there was a "sea east,"[324] and since we know that the earliest civilization had its origin in the central portion of what we now call North America, a "sea east" would be in the region of our present Atlantic Ocean.

This sea is referred to a second time in the record of Enoch: "There also came up a land out of the depth of the sea and so great was the fear of the enemies of the people of God, that they fled and stood afar off and went upon the land which came up out of the depth of the sea."[325]

322   Luke 3:5.
323   D&C 133:23-24.
324   Moses 6:42.
325   Moses 7:14.

Since there was a "sea east" in ancient times, there will undoubtedly be a similar body of water during the Millennium to fulfill the promise that the earth will become "like as it was before it was divided."

In that event America would then be the eastern-most portion of the continent of land which would extend almost around the earth. This would seem to give significance to the statement in Genesis that God planted a garden "eastward in Eden."[326] If a solid belt of land stretched across the area now occupied by the Pacific Ocean so that America was connected with Eurasia, it can be readily appreciated that the center of the United States would then be a land "eastward." Modern revelation has disclosed that this is exactly where the Garden of Eden was located.[327]

The Earth to Bring Forth Its Strength

Then the earth will bring forth its strength. Great forests will grow up in the wilderness.[328] Rivers and springs will change deserts and wastelands into meadows and farmlands.[329] Noxious weeds, briers and thorns will give way to groves, orchards and profitable plant life.[330]

The physical and chemical nature of the earth will also be quickened. The change will be so great that the Lord speaks of it as "a new earth" and says there will be so little to remind one of the deficient and fallen sphere which we now inhabit that "it shall not be remembered nor come to mind."[331]

---

326 Genesis 2:8.
327 Matthias F. Cowley, Wilford Woodruff, p. 481.
328 Isaiah 41:19.
329 Isaiah 35:7.
330 Isaiah 55:13.
331 Isaiah 65:17-19.

The refinement of the earth at that time will be so marked that the planet is described as being "transfigured." When the Apostles were together on the mount they were shown the vision of it and not at any time since then has the full account of its glory been revealed.[332]

No Sorrow among the Righteous Because There Will Be No Death

Not only will the earth be transfigured, but among the righteous even human life will function on a more perfect and efficient scale than at any time since the Fall. In Section 101 of the Doctrine and Covenants, one of the most singular prophecies in all holy writ is recorded. Speaking of the time of the Millennium it says: "and there shall be no sorrow because there is no death."[333] The implications of this promise are tremendous. Such a condition would require strict self-discipline among all human beings and a sufficiently strong control over natural phenomena and secular circumstances so that there would be no accidents, no disease, no infant mortality, no senile old age, and no congenital deformities. Such a condition would change many things in our mode of existence -- no funerals, no cemeteries, no mortuaries, and no insurance companies.

In saying that there be no death, however, the Lord does not mean that people living during the Millennium will be immortal. He goes on to explain that this promise simply means that among the righteous there will be no separation of the body from the spirit -- no consignment of the body to the grave.[334] Men will live until they are a hundred years old[335] in the full strength of the ancient patriarchs, then they

---

332   D&C 63:21.
333   D&C 101:29.
334   D&C 101:30-31; 63:51.
335   Isaiah 65:20.

will be changed in the twinkling of an eye from mortal to resurrected beings.[336] Such persons will be "caught up" and their rest will be glorious.[337]

Nor does the Lord imply that this blessed promise of "no death" applies to everyone. It only applies to the righteous and obedient. During at least the early part of the Millennium there will be many who will survive the great destruction who are not members of Christ's Kingdom and these will have the opportunity to hear the Gospel and join the Church if they so desire.[338] If they do not, however, but choose to remain in their sins, Isaiah clearly indicates that the sorrows of death are still theirs.[339]

The scripture also indicates that among the righteous there will be no juvenile crime, no disobedient or disrespectful youth. For, says the Lord, "their children shall grow up without sin unto salvation."[340] In the same place he states that the Saints will "multiply and wax strong." It is highly possible that with the cessation of war, the eradication of infant mortality, the increase of the human life span to one hundred years and the marked increase in the arable land area, the number of individuals who will populate the earth during the thousand years of the Millennial reign will total more than all those who lived on the earth during the previous six thousand years.

All Enmity to Cease

Another of the rather startling predictions of changes to come during the Millennium is the prophecy that animals will lose their enmity one toward another. Isaiah twice

336 D&C 63:51.
337 D&C 101:31.
338 D&C 77:11.
339 Isaiah 65:20.
340 D&C 45:58.

describes this phenomenon and makes it definitely clear that "the wolf also shall dwell with the lamb, and the leopard shall lie down with the kid; and the calf and the young lion and the fatling together."[341] He even goes further and predicts that the animal species which have formerly been classified as "carnivorous" because of their dependence on flesh from other animals will thereafter become herbivorous so that they can exist upon plant life rather than meat: "The lion shall eat straw like the bullock; and dust shall be the serpent's meat. They shall not hurt nor destroy in all my holy mountain saith the Lord."[342] In another place he again refers to this biological change when he says: "The lion shall eat straw like the ox."[343]

Not only will enmity between members of the animal kingdom disappear but fear and enmity between men and animals will likewise cease. Referring to it, Isaiah says: "And the sucking child shall play on the hole of the asp, and the weaned child shall put his hand on the cockatrice's den. They shall not hurt nor destroy in all my holy mountain."[344]

Enmity between individuals will also be eliminated. For centuries political scientists have dreamed of the unprecedented progress which mankind could make if their investments of money and materials could be directed exclusively toward peaceful pursuits. In the Millennium this will occur. Speaking of the relationship between individuals and nations, Isaiah says: "They shall beat their swords into plowshares, and their spears into pruning hooks; nation shall not lift up sword against nation, neither shall they learn war anymore."[345]

---

341   Isaiah 11:6-9; 65:25; Hosea 2:18.
342   Isaiah 65:25.
343   Isaiah 11:7.
344   Isaiah 11:8, 9.
345   Isaiah 2:4.

All People to Speak One Language

One of the great social stumbling blocks in this the twentieth century is our inability to communicate freely with the people of other nations. Language has degenerated into thousands of dialects and a man who can speak or understand even six or seven is considered a scholarly expert.

The reign of confusion which began with the confounding of tongues at the Tower of Babel still prevails. The only successful attempt to overcome it has been the agreement among scientists to use two dead languages -- the Greek and the Latin -- for terms and appellations in the various branches of scientific study.

There are some who think language has evolved -- that it is improving and becoming more flexible and expressive. However, prominent scholars agree with the scriptures that the very opposite is the case.[346] Language has devolved.

Moses states that originally the children of men had a language which was "pure and undefiled,"[347] and that Adam and the early patriarchs taught the people to write this language in a form revealed by God himself.[348] This was the only language used by the people of that day and age.[349] Ether confirms this fact and states that when the confounding of tongues occurred at the Tower of Babel, Jared and his brother, Mahonri-Moriancumer, pleaded with the Lord not to confound their knowledge of this perfect language. Their prayers were answered and the Jaredites carried the original Adamic tongue with them in their migrations.[350]

346   See numerous references in Joseph Fielding Smith, The Way to Perfection, chapter 10.
347   Moses 6:6.
348   Moses 6:46.
349   Genesis 11:6.
350   Ether 1:35-37.

During the Millennium the pure language of Adam, which apparently is the language of heaven itself, will again be established among all nations. Speaking of this fact the Prophet Zephaniah states: "For then will I turn to the people a pure language that they may all call upon the name of the Lord, to serve him with one consent."[351]

Satan to be Bound

Nineteen centuries ago when Jesus was beginning his earthly ministry he commanded certain evil spirits to leave the afflicted bodies of two men. Immediately the spirits cried out and said: "What have we to do with thee, Jesus, thou Son of God? Art thou come hither to torment us before the time?"[352]

These spirits were referring to "the time" of the Millennium which is the occasion appointed by God when Satan and all his fallen hosts will be cut off from their association with the human family.[353] Lucifer and his multitude of evil companions are "the angels which kept not their first estate, but left their own habitation."[354] They are "the angels that sinned"[355] in the first estate and were therefore prohibited from having physical bodies in this, the second estate.[356]

Lucifer has an unholy ambition to overthrow the Kingdom of God. Isaiah accused him openly: "O Lucifer, son of the morning!... Thou hast said in thy heart: I will ascend into heaven, I will exalt my throne above the stars of God; I will sit also upon the mount of the congregation, in the sides of the north; I will ascend above the heights of the clouds; I will

351   Zephaniah 3:9.
352   Matthew 8:29.
353   D&C 88:110; 43:31; 45:55; 84:100.
354   Jude 1:6.
355   2 Peter 2:4.
356   Teachings of the Prophet Joseph Smith, pp. 305-306.

be like the Most High."[357]

In his divine economy God has tolerated Lucifer and his hosts for a season only. As the Prophet Lehi explained, he has allowed them to use their rebellious influence to test the human family:

"Wherefore, men are free according to the flesh; and all things are given them which are expedient unto man. And they are free to choose liberty and eternal life, through the great mediation of all men, or choose captivity and death according to the captivity and power of the devil; for he seeketh that all men might be miserable like unto himself."[358]

Satan has given himself over completely to the destruction of all things which are good. He has so perverted his own course of existence that he has become perpetually miserable and therefore finds satanic pleasure in provoking the whole human family to a similar state of discontent and misery. Those who respond to his tempting become his servants.[359]

Lucifer's presence on the earth is permitted only through the sufferance of his elder brother, Jesus Christ. Satan has no legal right here -- merely a temporary license. With the ushering in of the Millennium, that license expires.

For one thousand years he will have no influence. He cannot ensnare nor bring a railing accusation against any man whether living or dead. It may seem strange to some that Satan will be prohibited from operating even in the spirit world, but such is surely the ease. If he were excluded from the mortal sphere alone, he would not be "bound" but merely restricted. However, the fact that he will be cut

357   Isaiah 14:12-14.
358   2 Nephi 2:27.
359   D&C 29:40, 45; Jacob 3:11; Mosiah 16:5.

off from the spirit world as well as mortality accounts for the unhampered facility and speed with which the plan of salvation will be promulgated among the spirits "in prison" during the period of the Millennium.

Return of the Translated City of Enoch

With the beginning of the Millennial reign, Enoch and his people will return to the earth. Here indeed is a thrilling epic. Consider for a moment the miniature biography of this man.

Enoch was ordained to the Priesthood when he was twenty-five years of age.[360] When the Lord called him to be a prophet he hesitated to accept the call because he was "a lad" and was hated because he was "slow of speech."[361] But the Lord healed Enoch of his impediment and he became a mighty prophet, seer and revelator. Mountains actually moved from their places at his command; rivers actually turned from their courses; the very earth trembled "so great was the power of the language which God had given him.[362] He built a great city which he later defended as a valiant general in what was probably the first pitched battle in the history of the world.[363] He was the clerk of the conference called by Father Adam at Adam-ondi-Ahman three years before Adam's death. Enoch wrote the official record of this conference and placed it in a book along with other revelations. This compilation became known as the Book of Enoch.[364]

At the age of 430, he and all his city were translated and

---

360   D&C 107:48.
361   Moses 6:31.
362   Moses 7:18.
363   Moses 7:13.
364   D&C 107:57.

removed to another sphere of action.[365] At this time Enoch and the citizens of his city were refined to that degree of glory which is called Terrestrial and the place of their habitation was of the Terrestrial order. Since that time, Enoch and the Saints with him have been ministering angels to this and other planets.[366] Enoch has personally returned to this earth on several known occasions. Jude and Paul were ministered to by Enoch. They both enjoyed personal associations with him and received important phases of the Gospel from his teachings.[367]

At the time of the Second Coming, Enoch and his translated city will return to this planet in accordance with the promise of the Lord. In speaking of the wonderful reunion between the people of Enoch and the Saints who will be living upon the earth at that time, the Lord declared to Enoch: "Then shalt thou and all thy city meet them there, (the Saints of the New Jerusalem) and we will receive them into our bosom, and they shall see us; and we will fall upon their necks and they shall fall upon ours and we will kiss each other."[368]

Chronology of Events Ushering in the Millennium

Now that we have considered some of the conditions which will prevail during the Millennium, let us start at the beginning and examine the sequence of dramatic incidents which will usher in that glorious era.

On December 27, 1832, at Kirtland, Ohio, the Lord gave a revelation concerning these events which is the most detailed account in any scripture. After describing the period of preparation when all things will be in commotion, the

365   Moses 7:21, 69.
366   Teachings of the Prophet Joseph Smith, p. 170.
367   Teachings of the Prophet Joseph Smith, pp. 169-171.
368   Moses 7:63.

revelation says: "And immediately there shall appear a great sign in heaven, and all people shall see it together."[369] Following this sign, "Another angel shall sound his trumpet, saying: That great church, the mother of abominations, that made all nations drink of the wine of the wrath of her fornication, that persecuteth the Saints of God, that shed their blood -- she who sitteth upon many waters, and upon the islands of the sea -- behold, she is the tares of the earth; she is bound in bundles; her bands are made strong, no man can loose them; therefore, she is ready to be burned. And he shall sound his trump both long and loud, and all nations shall hear it."[370]

"And there shall be silence in heaven for the space of half an hour; and immediately after shall the curtain of heaven be unfolded, as a scroll is unfolded after it is rolled up, and the face of the Lord shall be unveiled. And the Saints that are upon the earth, who are alive, shall be quickened and caught up to meet him."[371]

This is the Second Advent of the Messiah. This is "the coming in the clouds of heaven"[372] which Jesus predicted to the Jewish High Priest just before the crucifixion. This is the great event which the Saints were told to look for earnestly.

Resurrection of the Dead

Then the scripture continues: "And they who have slept in their graves shall come forth, for their graves shall be opened; and they also shall be caught up to meet him in the midst of the pillar of heaven -- they are Christ's the first fruits."[373]

---

369   D&C 88:93.
370   D&C 88:94.
371   D&C 88:95-96.
372   Matthew 26:64.
373   D&C 88:97-98.

This is the first resurrection. It will be carried out under the direction of Michael, or Adam[374] our valiant patriarchal ancestor who will call forth his righteous descendants to possess their glorified, resurrected bodies."[375]

"And after this another angel shall sound, which is the second trump; and then cometh the redemption of those who are Christ's at his coming; who have received their part in that prison which is prepared for them, that they might receive the gospel, and be judged according to men in the flesh."[376] These are they who rejected the gospel when they heard it the first time while upon the earth. They were therefore held back in the spirit world until they could be taught it a second time and thereafter accept it. Confirming this, the Savior states that these are they "who received not the testimony of Jesus in the flesh, but afterwards received it. These are they who are honorable men of the earth who were blinded by the craftiness of men ... wherefore, they are bodies terrestrial."[377]

Thus, the two resurrections referred to above will bring forth four classes of people: the members of the Church,[378] those who died without the law,[379] those who had the law of the gospel taught to them but procrastinated their full acceptance of it until they reached the spirit world,[380] and all little children who died before they reached the age of accountability.[381]

These two resurrections comprise "the resurrection of

374   D&C 27:11.
375   D&C 29:26; 78:16.
376   D&C 88:99.
377   D&C 76:73-78.
378   D&C 76:64.
379   D&C 45:54.
380   D&C 88:99 plus 76:73-78.
381   Mosiah 15:21, 25

the just" as distinguished from "the resurrection of the un-
just" which will occur at the end of the Millennium.[382]

Calling Up All the Remaining Spirits of the Dead

As the Savior descends upon the earth with all the multitudes who are caught up to meet him, "another trump shall
sound, which is the third trump, and then come the spirits of
men who are judged and are found under condemnation."[383]
Then the scripture adds a significant postscript: "And these
are the rest of the dead."[384]

These are they who would not accept the gospel plan
either on earth or in the spirit world.[385] Even though they
might have admired those who lived the higher law, nevertheless they would not adopt it for themselves. They gloried
in the exploitation of the flesh and rejected the responsibili-
ties of life. "These are they who are liars and sorcerers, and
adulterers, and whoremongers, and whosoever loves and
makes a lie."[386] In the vision of it Joseph Smith declared: "We
saw ... they were as innumerable as the stars in the firmament of heaven, or as the sand upon the seashore."[387]

A Conference of the Entire Human Race at the Beginning of the Millennium

Here indeed will be the greatest congregation ever gathered together upon the face of the earth. Here will be all the
resurrected and the "spirits" of "the rest of the dead." Present in that vast assembly will be every single human being

382   D&C 76:17; 88:101.
383   D&C 88:100.
384   D&C 88:101.
385   D&C 76:82-85.
386   D&C 76:103.
387   D&C 76:109.

that ever lived upon this planet.

Then an angel who is identified elsewhere as Moroni[388] will stand before this mighty throng and proclaim: "Fear God and give glory to him who sitteth upon the throne forever and ever for the hour of his judgment is come!"[389]

As these words are uttered the righteous will have cause to rejoice, but the unresurrected spirits will quake with fear and trembling. As they reflect upon their surrounding circumstances they will realize that what they formerly deemed to be a mere superstition is in fact the most obvious eternal reality.

They will suddenly comprehend the reality of the existence of God in whose image they were made and whose Son is Jehovah, even he who was manifest in the flesh as Jesus Christ.[390] As this conviction strikes upon their hearts they will follow the righteous by falling upon their knees and confessing openly that their elder brother, Jesus Christ, is indeed the Savior of mankind.[391]

And then, while every knee in this vast assembly is bowed and every tongue is confessing the identity of their Messiah, another ambassador of the Lord will appear and speak forth triumphantly: "She is fallen who made all nations drink of the wine of the wrath of her fornication; she is fallen, is fallen!"[392] And another angel shall declare: "It is finished: it is finished! The Lamb of God has overcome, and trodden the winepress alone, even the winepress of the fierceness of the wrath of Almighty God."[393]

---

388   D&C 88:104 plus 133:36 and 20:6.
389   D&C 88:104.
390   John 1:1, 14.
391   D&C 88:104.
392   D&C 88:105.
393   D&C 88:106.

Then the Savior will acknowledge his Saints before this tremendous congregation and those who were despised and ridiculed while they lived upon the earth will be exalted before their former persecutors. Thus, these who were counted least among the kingdoms of men will be made first in the Kingdom of God.

The History of the World to be Revealed

Now the Lord will bring before this conference a marvelous revelation. He says he will show it to "all the living."[394] It will be the greatest spectacle that any of us will have ever seen -- a vision of the history of the world!

Every student of history knows what a thrilling experience it is to gain a familiar knowledge of things that are past, but all that one could learn in all the books that were ever written would not compare with what we shall learn when the Lord presents this all-searching panoramic revelation.

The Lord will show us a thousand years at a time, and we will have the opportunity of examining the lives of all those who lived in each period. The secret acts of men will be there for all to see -- even the secret intents of their hearts -- and many who thought their sins were cleverly hidden forever will see them blazoned forth -- shouted, as it were, from the very housetops.[395]

The secret acts of God will also be revealed and with Brigham Young we will be led to exclaim: "There is not one thing that the Lord could do for the salvation of the human family that he has neglected to do."[396]

As the sixth period of a thousand years is opened to our

394   D&C 88:108.
395   D&C 88:108-110.
396   Discourses of Brigham Young, p. 41.

gaze we shall finally see ourselves. And what a moment that will be! Even as those in past history will see themselves and their lives whether they were good or evil, so shall we see ours. Every detail will be there for all to scrutinize. How intense we shall be to see our own lives shown forth in vivid panorama. How thankful the Saints will be in that day for the principle of repentance and the ordinance of baptism for the remission of sins. Many are inclined to think of these principles as mere formalities for Church membership, but in the day of this great revelation the Saints will discover that all their mistakes and sins which they overcame and brought under the cleansing principle of the Atonement will be literally blotted out[397] and will not appear in the vision to condemn them. Then the Saints will rejoice in their God and be thankful that they listened to their authorities and endeavored from day to day to overcome their weaknesses and imperfections.

And the good things the Saints accomplished will be shown. The world will come to know that their humility was not their weakness but their strength. The secret acts of benevolence, the sacrifices for the cause of the Gospel, the sufferings which they patiently endured -- all these will be shown to their everlasting credit and honor.

This will be a vision of the history of the world as the Lord himself has seen it. And even while the Saints rejoice to see the reward of their faithfulness, the wicked shall have cause to mourn and lament for they shall see their lives exhibited for their true worth. They will be condemned by their filthy works, their lies, adulteries, conspiracies, their cruel acts and false philanthropies. Consider the fierce repentance of the wicked when they behold this searching revelation of their private lives and secret sins in mortality.

---

397   Alma 7:13.

The Judgment at the Beginning of the Millennium

Take note of the warning which Moroni will declare to the people: "Fear God ... for the hour of his judgment is come."[398]

It may be surprising to some that a judgment will be pronounced at the beginning of the Millennium. Usually we speak only of the judgment referred to by John[399] which comes at the end of the Millennium. But actually there are three. The first is when each person dies. His spirit is subjected to a judgment as soon as it crosses the veil.[400] The second is the judgment plainly referred to as occurring at the beginning of the Millennium,[401] and the third is the "final" judgment which follows a thousand years later.[402]

After the panoramic vision of the life we each lived has been exhibited, surely it will not be difficult to pronounce a true and equitable judgment upon the human race. As the Prophet Alma and the Prophet Jacob declared, we shall have a "bright recollection" of our past -- "a perfect knowledge of all our guilt and our uncleanness and our nakedness; and the righteous shall have a perfect knowledge of their enjoyment, and their righteousness, being clothed with purity."[403] Each individual "shall see eye to eye" with his neighbor and be known as he is known to himself. And each will go away to his own place -- to seek that level of society where he is most comfortable. "Behold, they are their own judges," says

---

398   D&C 88:104.
399   Revelation 20:12.
400   Alma 40:11-13.
401   D&C 29:12.
402   Revelation 20:12.
403   Alma 11:43; 2 Nephi 9:14.

Alma.[404]

But a judgment is not only to condemn. It is also to reward. And this particular judgment is especially designed to point out those who are ready at the beginning of the Millennium to receive their salvation and, insofar as possible, their exaltation. Speaking of this occasion the scripture says: "And then ... the Saints shall be filled with his glory and receive their inheritance and be made equal with him."[405] As the Lord receives his chosen Saints unto himself he will commemorate this triumphant event by partaking of the sacrament with them just as he did with his disciples at the Last Supper.[406] Then he will ordain them to go forth and establish a just government upon all the face of the earth.[407]

Establishing a Just Government upon All the Earth

It can be readily visualized that the passing of events as previously described will cause all sovereign functions of government to automatically gravitate toward the King of Kings and Lord of Lords whose right it is to reign. He will establish a single kingdom[408] -- a perfect theocracy.[409]

He will commence his work by sending forth 144,000 ambassadors to teach principles of righteousness to all who survived the pre-Millennial cleansing of the earth.[410] The principles of theocratic government will then be established. It will emphasize individual self-control rather than bureaus and agencies to enforce control. It will promote righteous-

---

404   Alma 41:7.
405   D&C 88:107.
406   D&C 27:5-14; Luke 22:18.
407   Revelation 20:6.
408   Daniel 2:44.
409   See James E. Talmage, Articles of Faith, p. 363.
410   D&C 77:11.

ness rather than legislate it. There will be a uniform world-wide application of all laws and administrative policies with two great world capitals from which the supervisory functions of government will go forth.[411]

All genius and energy, government, economics and social science will be geared to a single aim -- the comfort, refinement, instruction and improvement of the human family. The regulation of affairs, righteously administered by humble servants of the Priesthood, will provide at last the Utopian perfection for which men have dreamed and died down through the centuries. In an atmosphere of harmony and achievement there will be neither armies nor navies, prisons nor policemen -- only judges, schools and temples.

Neither Atheists nor Agnostics during the Millennium

For all who dwell on the earth during the thousand years of peace there will be no shadow of ignorance concerning the reality of God or the purpose of his plans for the welfare of the race. As has been previously pointed out, at the very beginning of the Millennium every knee shall bow and every tongue confess that Jesus is the Christ -- for in that day they shall see with their own eyes and marvel at his glory. They may not all agree to immediately accept the divine commandments of God -- but neither will they be able to claim agnostic ignorance concerning his existence. Speaking of this fact the Prophet Jeremiah declared: "And they shall teach no more every man his neighbor and every man his brother, saying: Know the Lord, for they shall know me, from the least of them unto the greatest of them."[412] And Nephi added: "the earth shall be full of the knowledge of the Lord as the waters cover the sea."[413]

411   D&C 133:21.
412   Jeremiah 31:34.
413   2 Nephi 30:15.

All prayers will receive a direct and prompt response. In fact, the Lord told the Prophet Isaiah that "before they call, I will answer, and while they are yet speaking, I will hear."[414] "In that day whatsoever any man shall ask shall be given him."[415]

All Things to be Revealed

During the Millennium the "glass darkly"[416] spoken of by Paul which beclouds the perspective of mortal men will be removed and we shall come to know and understand all things. "Yea, verily, I say unto you, in that day when the Lord shall come, he shall reveal all things -- things which have passed, and hidden things which no man knew."[417]

Among these treasures to be revealed will be many of the ancient scriptures which have been lost. The Lord specifically promises that all of them will be revealed. Among these will be included: the Book of Enoch,[418] the Brass Plates of Laban,[419] the scriptures of the Lost Ten Tribes,[420] the prophetic history of the world by Mahonri-Moriancumer,[421] and many other lost scriptures too numerous to mention. As Nephi taught, "Wherefore, all things which have been revealed unto the children of men shall at that day be revealed."[422]

All of those things which we have secretly longed to know will be disclosed. It will be a day in which "nothing shall be withheld, whether there be one God or many gods,

414   Isaiah 65:24.
415   D&C 101:27.
416   1 Corinthians 13:12.
417   D&C 101:32, 33.
418   D&C 107:57.
419   Alma 37:3-4.
420   2 Nephi 29:11-14.
421   Ether 4:6-7 plus 2 Nephi 27:7-9.
422   2 Nephi 30:18.

they shall be manifest, all thrones and dominions, princi-
palities and powers, shall be revealed ... and also, if there be
bounds set to the heavens or to the seas, or to the dry land,
or to the sun, moon or stars."[423]

The Science of Astronomy to be taught by Revelation

Anyone who has sat beneath the dome of an astronomical observatory and gazed through the lenses of a giant tele-
scope will realize the inestimable worth of a revelation on
the science of astronomy. The vast proportions of this field
of research are comparatively unexplored by man; therefore
the Lord has promised that he will teach it to us in his own
way. It will probably be like the vision which God gave to
Abraham when he said: "And I show these things unto you,
Abraham, before you go into Egypt that you might declare
all these things unto them." Thus, we shall learn, just as the
teacher of the Egyptians, what the relation is between our
own solar system and the rest of the galaxy of which we are
a part. We shall pierce the radius of our Heavenly Father's
astronomical kingdom and see Kolob, the governing one --
the great central dynamo -- through which all the rest of our
galaxy receives its light and power.[424]

We shall see the other governing spheres and learn the
science of mathematics by which they maintain their times,
seasons and order. Men who called themselves astronomers
while they lived upon the earth, will, in that day, marvel
as they behold the secrets of the heavens which their most
powerful telescopes and their most sensitive photographic
plates could not disclose or detect. Surely, they shall praise
the name of the Omnipotent Elohim in that day for in this
revelation they will behold their God moving in his eternal
majesty and power.

423   D&C 121:28-30.
424   Abraham 3:3.

Speaking of the scope of this promised revelation, the Lord said: "All the times of their revolutions, all the appointed days, months and years ... and all their glories, laws, and set times, shall be revealed in the days of the dispensation of the fullness of times."[425]

The Science of Geology to be taught by Revelation

And in another place the scripture says: "Verily I say unto you, in that day when the Lord shall come, he shall reveal all things -- things which have passed, and hidden things which no man knew, things of the earth, by which it was made, and the purpose and the end thereof ... things that are in the earth, and upon the earth."[426]

Much time and effort has been expended by students of both science and religion to determine from their respective authorities what pattern of existence the earth passed through before it became a fit habitation for man. The scientist has gone to "the record of the rocks." The student of religion has gone to the scriptures -- to the recorded testimony of the earth's creator.

But surprisingly enough, the Lord has never revealed -- or at least it isn't recorded -- what the pattern of this earth's mortal "creation" really was. The "creation" in Genesis and the Pearl of Great Price makes no reference to our present planetary home. As the Book of Moses clearly indicates[427] and the Church authorities have consistently taught, the so-called "creation" has reference to the pattern of construction followed in the organizing of the premortal sphere which we occupied in the First Estate. In all existing accounts the Lord deliberately by-passes the subject of the earth's mortal

425   D&C 121:28-31.
426   D&C 101:32-34.
427   Moses 3:4-5.

creation.

The Lord's revelation at the beginning of the Millennium will therefore be new knowledge for the student of the scriptures as well as the student of science.

As we behold the true genesis of the earth we may marvel to find out how much of the true story our students of geology were able to unravel; or, on the other hand, we may discover that the accepted theories of the earth's creation were in fact as naive and child-like as the superstitions of the dark ages seem to us now. Of this we may be sure, however, that all the truth relating to the creation will finally be reconciled -- whether it was discovered by science or revealed to a prophet.

And those students who made a sincere effort to find out the truth through science will know that their scholarship and painstaking effort were not in vain, for they will be all the more appreciative of the revelation and comprehend its significance all the more easily. The faith of the Saints will likewise be vindicated. They who had the faith to believe what little the Lord has given to his prophets on this subject will have cause to rejoice on this occasion. Though they were laughed upon in their own generation and were called "foolish, superstitious and unscholarly" for believing the word of the Lord, yet will they be honored when the Master Architect shows forth the true science of geology in a visual demonstration of what actually occurred.

Sons of Levi to Make an Offering to the Lord in Righteousness

This will also be the time when an event will take place to which John the Baptist made reference when he restored the Aaronic Priesthood. He said: "And this (the Aaronic

Priesthood) shall never be taken again from the earth until the sons of Levi do offer again an offering unto the Lord in righteousness."[428]

The occasion for this predicted "offering" is described in great detail by the Prophet Ezekiel. In fact, it comprises the last nine chapters of his recorded words. He was shown the magnificent temple which the Jews would build in preparation for the Messiah's coming; and he saw the sons of Levi who would be chosen from among the returning hosts of Israel to offer sacrifices on the altars of the temple. From Ezekiel's description it is plain that these "sacrifices" will be identical with those offered by the sons of Levi in ancient times.

After the sons of Levi have made an acceptable offering to the Lord, Ezekiel saw that "the glory of the Lord came into the house by the way of the gate whose prospect is toward the east.... And the glory of the Lord filled the house."[429] "Then said the Lord unto me; This gate shall be shut, it shall not be opened, and no man shall enter in by it; because the Lord, the God of Israel, hath entered in by it."[430]

Immediately the name of Jerusalem will be changed. The meaning of the new name will be, "The Lord is there."[431]

For some time the ancient sacrifices under the Law of Moses will be offered by the Priests of Levi in a spirit of righteous thanksgiving.[432] The Levite Priests of early days subverted the offerings of the temple with idolatrous practices,[433] but of the Levite Priests in the last days the Lord

---

428 D&C 13.
429 Ezekiel 43:4-5.
430 Ezekiel 44:2.
431 Ezekiel 48:35.
432 Ezekiel 43:18-27.
433 Ezekiel 44:10, 12.

had this to say: "They shall enter into my sanctuary and they shall come near to my table, to minister unto me, and they shall keep my charge."[434]

That these Levitical ordinances will not continue for long would appear from the words John the Baptist when he said the Aaronic or Levitical Priesthood would be dissolved as a separate function from the Higher Priesthood as the sons of Levi offered an offering of righteousness unto the Lord. Then the temple in Jerusalem will be used for the ordinances and sealing work of the Higher Priesthood. This is made clear by the statement that in "Zion, and in her stakes and in Jerusalem ... shall be the places for the baptisms for your dead."[435] The verses immediately following indicate that this is not only referring to baptisms for the dead but also the higher temple ordinances.[436]

The Millennial Era Established

Thus will the Millennial reign be inaugurated upon the earth. The following thousand years will be the busy, sweeping climax to man's probation or "second estate." It will be a golden era of peace. A day when the whole earth will become a garden of luxurious foliage and abundant harvests. Every creature in the animal kingdom will become the friend and comforter of man. Among the human race a universal brotherhood will become an accomplished reality. Beautiful, well planned cities will stretch like jewels around the earth and the spires of holy temples will rise as shafts of tabernacled glory to show forth the hope of the Lord for the living and the dead.

Such is the prophetic destiny of this earth and its inhabitants in the day when the trumpets of the angels shall pro-

434   Ezekiel 44:15.
435   D&C 124:36.
436   D&C 124:37-39.

claim the ushering in of the great Millennial reign of Jesus Christ on earth!

Made in the USA
Lexington, KY
20 December 2014